STUDIO ESSENTIALS

BY TOM HAPKE

Cover art by Levin Pfeufer

Cherry Lane Music Company
Educational Director/Project Supervisor: Susan Poliniak
Director of Publications: Mark Phillips
Publications Coordinator: Rebecca Skidmore
Assistant Editor: Natalie Chomet

ISBN 978-1-60378-049-0

EXCLUSIVELY DISTRIBUTED BY

HAL•LEONARD®
CORPORATION
7777 W. BLUEMOUND RD. P.O. BOX 13819 MILWAUKEE, WI 53213

Visit our website at www.cherrylaneprint.com

CONTENTS

ABOUT THIS BOOK

The product names, designations, and circuits specified in this book are mostly trademarked and/or patented. Although we have taken the greatest care in the checking of information (both text and illustrations), such information changes and errors cannot always be avoided. The publisher and author assume no responsibility for incorrect data and their consequences.

Graphics by Thomas Schad (3D Graphics) and Marco Besler (Vektor Graphics).

Photos by Marco Besler.

Editorial work (German version) by André Inderfurth, Patrick Lemmens, Roland Stearns, Fritz Fey, Johannes Siegler, Klaus Gehlhaar, Pascal Miguet, and Mike Kahsnitz.

Certain photos used with the kind permission of KSdigital, AKG, Neumann, SPL, Sommercable, RTW, Neutrik, Galaxy Studios (Belgium), Primacoustic, and Mega Audio.

English translation by Roland Stearns and Tira Neal.

PREFACE

A request from my publisher for a book on recording technology and studio work was the origin of *Studio Essentials*. It was a rather attractive proposal, so despite the complexities of such an enormous subject, I accepted. I have spent half of my life in recording studios working as a songwriter, studio musician, and producer. In fact, my desire to make high-quality recordings of my music inspired me to build three studios. My experiences with studio building, recording equipment, and techniques have gone into this book.

Studio Essentials describes complex topics in simple language, and is geared toward a practice-orientated approach to recording studio arts. I have tried to take into consideration the complete range of the music production experience from the first stirrings of a song idea to the creation of a finished master recording.

What makes this book special is the help of my colleagues—including experts from the studio domain and the world of sound product development—who contributed invaluable technical advice. I hope that *Studio Essentials* will provide you with an instructive overview into the studio world, and will motivate you and help you to improve your skills in this great and exciting area.

– *Tom Hapke*

ACKNOWLEDGMENTS

I want to open-heartedly thank those who worked on this project, and who stood by me and had faith in this baby during the two years of its production—a deep bow to you all.

I am much obliged to my co-author Marco Besler, the man who always stood by this project like no other. His contributions have helped make *Studio Essentials* what it is. Thank you for your over-whelming support!

Marco Besler and Tom Hapke

I also want to thank the following people: Beata Mablad, Sandra Menzel, Sylvia Pick, Martina Hapke, Birgit Büring, Jens Vollmer, Christian Schneider, my jam colleague Dominik Krämer, Cosmas Cösters, Dirko Juchem, Wolfgang Hoffmann, Ralph Vogler, Silvia Dias, Nadja Tolles, Mathias Conrad, Vinnie Leyh, Markus Born, Florian Sitzmann, Bettina Besler, Mark Laukel, Uwe Ruppel, Armin Weis, Thomas Barth, Freddy Scheffenacker, and, of course, my family.

ROOM ACOUSTICS

What Are Acoustics?

The term *acoustics* refers to the way a sound from some source is reflected or returned in a given space. Humans need acoustics in order to orient themselves to their surroundings.

Anechoic Room

This is a room that has practically no reflections and no reverberation for frequencies under 100 Hz. Microphone manufacturers use such rooms for tests and design measurements. If you close your eyes in such a room, it is possible to completely lose your sense of balance because this needs acoustic reference to function. The ear needs reflections for orientation, and these do not exist in a large enough quantity in such a room.

What Are Reflections?

Reflections are returned sound waves, usually from hard surfaces in a given area (for example, the walls in a house). The path of a signal radiates in all directions from a so-called *point source*, and the definition applies even when this point is smaller than the wavelength itself. The harder the reflecting surfaces are, the more that arriving wave energy will be returned in the form of reflections. A law of reflected sound states that the angle of arrival equals the angle of reflection.

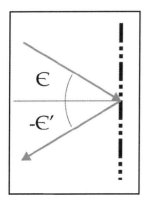

Early Reflections

These are reflections that arrive from the nearest surfaces (walls, for example).

Tip: One of the easiest ways to determine where the early reflections first appear is to sit in your main listening spot and have a second person walk along the side wall of the room with a mirror. The point where you first see the speaker reflected in the mirror is where the early reflection ricochets. This follows the above law of reflected sound.

Late Reflections

These are considered to be reflections from more distant surfaces. They are a major part of a room's total reflection pattern, which establishes a distinct sonic "ambiance." The way these reflections build up and are perceived is dependent upon how the room is "excited." The stronger the impulse (i.e., attack) of a signal that is released into a room, the more definitively one can recognize and categorize that room's acoustic character.

Tip: A fast and effective method of obtaining a general impression of a room's acoustic properties is simply to clap your hands while moving about the room. The sound of clapping has a very strong impulse character. This method will quickly reveal the room's reflective characteristics. Flutter echo and shadow reverb, if present, will also be immediately detected using this method.

Flutter Echo

A *flutter echo* is a series of reflected impulses emanating from a specific source that causes distinct (non-diffuse) reflections. Waves are bounced back and forth, creating the impression of a series of diminishing echoes. This is especially noticeable with sounds that have a strong impulse character (clapping, etc.). These echoes are, for the most part, very disturbing elements in any listening or recording situation. Flutter echo is especially problematic when two parallel walls are spaced so that other reflective surfaces are minimized in relation to these "echo walls." To eliminate flutter echo, the engineer should either try to dampen one of the offending surfaces by hanging some kind of absorptive material (fabric, for example), or redirect echoes to less acoustically problematic locations with the help of diffusers (for example, large, movable walls). Simply changing microphone or performer location can also often eliminate flutter echo.

Reverberation

This very familiar term describes the diffuse mix of individual reflections that becomes denser over time. It is a result of reflections that continue to repeat until their energy is gradually dissipated.

Standing Waves

Standing waves are a phenomenon that can often occur in rooms with two or more parallel surfaces. Depending on room size and signal frequency, a wave sounding between these walls can peak at one stationary (or standing) point, and resonate constantly in that location until it dies out. In any case, this is not a desirable acoustic situation.

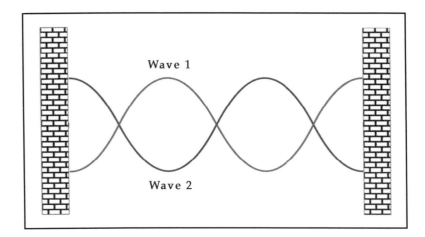

Standing waves occur when a wavelength of a specific frequency (as can be seen in the graphic) corresponds to the distance between two walls, creating a cyclical, one-location buildup. This situation may be described as the superimposition of two positive signal phases that (falsely) amplifies the signal to the point of "boominess." Most of the time this problem occurs in small rooms—particularly in the lower frequencies—and is termed *room modality*, which is another way of referring to the natural resonances of a room. As stated above, this phenomenon is linked to room size and frequencies with wavelengths that match the distances between the reflecting surfaces. The applicable mathematical formula is as follows.

λ = wavelength = c / f

c = wave velocity in air (c = 343 meters per second in 20° Celsius/68° Fahrenheit)

f = frequency (in Hz = 1 cycle per second)

Here's another way of stating it:

343 / room length in meters = standing wave frequency

Any kind of object used to deflect or interrupt a standing wave must be considerably larger than the wavelength itself. Therefore, lower-frequency waves are difficult to eliminate (for example, a 50 Hz wave is 22.5 feet long), while those in the middle or higher frequencies are much easier to control.

The so-called *shutter echo* is a type of standing wave that may be eliminated with relative ease, as it typically has a higher frequency and, thus, a shorter wavelength.

The Comb Filter Effect

While a studio monitor sends its signal directly to a recording engineer's ear, another portion of the wave may arrive reflected from a worktable or mixer. When this occurs, there will be different arrival times (i.e., phase shifts) that cause parts of these superimposed waves to cancel each other out. When this problem is graphically depicted on a computer monitor or other display, these cancellations resemble the fine teeth on a comb—hence the name.

Unfortunately, this is a problem that cannot always be eliminated entirely, but it can be reduced. The goal is to zero in on the direct signal while avoiding any reflections from surface areas that can be problematic.

How to Avoid the Comb Filter Effect

Shorter waves tend to be dispersed through the complex topography of the mixing console (knobs, faders), which creates a kind of diffusing surface. Most mixers are also built with a downward slanting top, which redirects any tendency for comb effects toward the lower body and away from ear level.

A deep working table is an inherently problematic reflecting surface and should be avoided. You can also place a lot of objects on your worktable to aid in sound diffusion (good news for messy engineers!). Also, the placement of the video monitor should not be too high.

What Makes a Room "Good" or "Bad"?

In order for a room to be acoustically "good," it must have an even, gradual dissipation of a sound's entire frequency spectrum, with no individual reflections audible. The first reflections are decisive in creating the perception of room size; in this respect, reverberation is much less important. What remains is a diffuse mix of room reflections that build up according to a room's sonic characteristics. The more even such reflections are, the more pleasant a room's reverb qualities are perceived to be. High frequencies die out rather faster than lower frequencies, in part owing to the latter's greater wavelength and energy. The reverb time of lower frequencies is usually greater than that of higher frequencies.

Options for Improving a Room's Acoustics

Room Proportions

Rooms with wall and ceiling surfaces that are of the same height, width, and depth are "terrific" if you wish to constantly battle with standing waves. But it is possible to improve rooms with proportional problems. For example, one can change measurements by adding a wall section—but do so, please, with massive, absorptive material. The room proportions should not be divided up solely to avoid standing waves.

Microphone Use

In a problematic room, one should consider simply putting each microphone nearer to its sound source, thus minimizing the effect of room acoustics. Later, one can add room ambience electronically, or more consistent "machine acoustics." Keep this principle in mind: The more direct a signal is, the less a possibly problematic ambient acoustic will be likely to interfere with it.

Room-Building Basics

Room dimensions (height, width, and depth) should be varied so that any possible problems with low-frequency sounds are minimized at the outset. One (deadly) counterexample would consist of parallel walls, parallel ceiling and floor, and walls that are equal in length.

Avoid at all costs large, reflective, unbroken wall surfaces. Also avoid smooth, reflecting floor and ceiling surfaces—for example, wood, glass, and concrete. Be careful to choose acoustically "suitable" furnishings.

Speakers (i.e., monitors) should be placed to follow basic stereo monitoring rules of thumb (see *Sound Formats*, page 66).

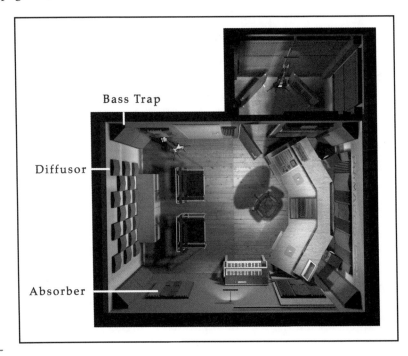

Many acoustic element manufacturers offer brief professional consulting sessions to those who are planning and building recording spaces. One of these consultants, upon receiving your room dimensions, may be able to suggest acoustical extras to improve things. In cases where budget is a concern, such consultations need target only those improvements that are most needed.

Acoustical Elements

There are many items with which a studio designer can improve the acoustic qualities of a room.

Diffusers

Early reflections play a big part in our perception of room size. A diffuser can increase the amount of diffracted sound, making it difficult to determine a room's size. Smaller rooms that deliver a very short reverb time can be improved with diffusers—they can help to eliminate cues about the room's small size.

Moreover, positively- or negatively-phased waves may superimpose themselves on each other, creating undesirable cancellations or emphasis. Flutter echoes are caused by strong, discernible, non-diffused wall reflections. Through their ability to disperse such waves, diffusers may also be effective against these problems. The bottom line is that absorption and reflection produce diffusion. In the simplest of cases, one may employ wooden slats in various sizes and thicknesses fastened to a rear wall so that about half of the surface is covered, and few (if any) reflective surfaces remain exposed.

Absorbers

An *absorber* functions as a complementary opposite to a diffuser, and is usually constructed from porous foam. However, carpeting and curtains made from heavy materials—even plants—can also fit the bill. Used in quantity, absorbers can deaden a room completely, since such material can absorb virtually all of a signal's frequencies.

Depending on the type of absorber, however, reverberation above a certain frequency can also fall victim to absorption while other frequencies may remain relatively untouched. Outfitting a room with only absorbers will shift the relationship between higher and lower frequencies to the point at which a lackluster, "boomy" room is created—lower frequencies retain their reverberation, and highs have little or no chance of being heard. Pyramid-shaped absorbers are not recommended for deadening a room because their absorption is too frequency-dependent.

Normally, an absorber is placed in a room location where first reflections appear (see *Early Reflections* on page 11). Absorbers should be placed about 50 centimeters both above and below ear level. Other popular absorber locations are on the ceiling and above the mixing console.

Bass Traps

These acoustic devices should be used where there is a need to absorb lower frequencies. They are mostly round in shape, or corner-angled columns made from material appropriate for swallowing up frequencies between 20 and 500 Hz.

Bass traps, as implied above, are best suited for room corners where lower frequencies propagate. As this bass wave buildup is strongest in room corners, one becomes more aware of the effect when listening there. Other significant wave buildups may occur at the halfway point between two corners. The closer a room is to having four equal sides, the greater such low-frequency wave buildups follow the tendencies mentioned above.

These wave buildups are displaced wherever walls are not parallel. In any case, an absorber functions best when placed right at the point or in the middle of one of these wave buildups.

Acoustic Differences Between Recording and Production or Mastering Rooms

Acoustically, there is no real difference between production and mastering rooms. In both workplaces, the goal is be able to decide quickly which sonic changes (highs, mids, lows, loudness), if any, are correct (i.e., true to their original sound), and which are not.

Optimal Recording Room Properties

The recording room should be constructed so as to leave crucial factors—such as reverberation time (decay time) and room frequency response characteristics—open for variation.

Note that a room's spatial qualities may determine which instrument(s) may be recorded there successfully; room acoustics should be suited to the instrument being recorded. If the studio budget allows it, the aspiring owner should consider having more than one room, each for different recording purposes as designated by each room's reverberation time.

Reverberation Times

This is the value expressed by the industry designation "RT60" (RT = reverb time). This refers to the amount of time needed for a signal to decay by 60 dB below its first appearance. For example, a reverb time of 0.3 seconds means that the room maintains a sound for 0.3 seconds before it reaches 60 dB below its initial level.

Recording Room Reverberation Times

At this stage the musical style becomes as important—or more so—than room specifics. Values of 0.8 to 1.2 seconds are good for a wide variety of chamber music, rock, and jazz; 1.8 seconds is very pleasant for a choral recording.

Production and Mastering Room Reverberation Times

A recommended reverb time in a smaller production room is about 0.2 seconds, extending in larger rooms up to 0.3 seconds. These parameters typically make one feel acoustically "at home." They enable one to maintain a fairly impartial sonic judgment with regard to any added reverb, which is important because the perceived sonic qualities of a room strongly influence how an engineer applies this and other effects. There are measuring tools that can help to determine a room's reverb time.

Wave Shielding and Room-Within-a-Room Construction

In planning a studio, one cannot ignore the need to protect the environment from unwanted sonic interference. This means keeping sound from entering and escaping a given space, whether by transmission through the air or via solid material. This is important because recording and production rooms are often near each other.

The best protection is provided by firm, airtight construction and the use of massive materials. Ground vibration may be halted by heavy carpeting or clay flooring that may rest on a sand-based underpinning. Air waves become ground waves when, for example, they are picked up and further transmitted by walls. Perhaps the best way to provide wave shielding is by building an insulated room-within-a-room.

Room-within-a-room construction enables recordists and production personnel to carry on simultaneous recording and mixing sessions without sound leaking into neighboring rooms or facilities. This has nothing to do with room acoustics—it's just pure and simple wave shielding.

The supporting structure and insulation should ensure that the inner room has essentially no acoustic contact with its outer, shielding counterpart. In other words, they are "de-coupled."

Microphone Characteristics—Some General Points

Simply put, the job of a microphone is to convert sound waves (air movement) into electrical signals. In most cases, this is achieved through a vibrating membrane responding to air movements, which are in turn converted into correspondingly variable electrical impulses.

Types of Microphone Patterns

Omnidirectional-Pattern Microphones

An *omnidirectional-pattern* (*omni* for short) microphone is one that generally records sound waves equally and independently, regardless of their point of origin. Another important feature of the omni is that it exhibits no *proximity effect* (a tendency to boost bass frequencies as a sound source moves closer), as opposed to, say, a cardioid-pattern microphone. One can sing as close to an omni mic as one wishes and the resulting sound should be very natural, without any bass emphasis. Omni mics are, however, less discriminating—they tend to pick up everything, including room acoustics and, unfortunately, unwanted noises. However, a decisive advantage of the omni is its ability to lend breadth and atmosphere to a recording, which are indispensible elements. The omni is a multitalented performer and is relatively immune to problematic vocal "popping."

Cardioid-Pattern Microphones

The *cardioid-pattern* microphone is highly sensitive to sounds toward its front and least sensitive to sounds from behind. Microphones such as the cardioid are also described as *directional*—another way of saying that they are more sensitive to sounds coming from one direction over another. Generally, cardioid mics should face a sound source directly. They are often a popular choice for recording because in small rooms they can minimize acoustically inappropriate reflections and other unwanted sounds. Their ambient pickup is typically half that of the omni, and this can be beneficial in less-than-ideal acoustical situations. Cardioids, too, are multitalented, and are a kind of complementary opposite to omnis, as they can bring a signal "nearer." A directional microphone such as a cardioid can, however, exhibit proximity effect.

Hypercardioid-Pattern Microphones

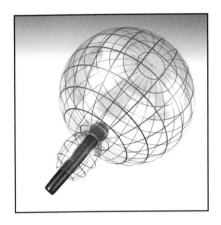

These mics carry the cardioid concept one step further, with a narrow pickup pattern that allows for even greater focus on a sound source. Hypercardioids are ideal for recording situations in which a smaller recording "window" is needed (to isolate the sound of a tom in a drum kit, for example) to reduce bleed-through from neighboring instruments.

Figure Eight–Pattern Microphones

The recording field of a *figure eight–pattern* microphone is comprised of two diametrically opposed cardioid patterns in opposite directions (i.e., 180 degrees out of phase with each other). If one does not anticipate many highly similar voice ranges (i.e., voices of the same type, and singing in the same frequency range), which could cancel one another out, one may use this placed in between, say, a singer and a chorus or background group.

The Proximity Effect

Generally speaking, for a clean studio recording one should maintain a distance of about 30 centimeters between a microphone and a sound source. The correct placement of a pop shield can often create the proper distance automatically. At distances closer than 30 centimeters, proximity effect becomes a factor, causing stronger bass reinforcement as a sound source moves nearer to the microphone. A solution to this, when available, is the microphone's low cut switch, which rolls off the bass beginning at 60, 80, 100, or 120 Hz, depending on the mic's pattern. Bass frequencies below the chosen frequency can drop off sharply. Used, for example, with the near miking of an acoustic guitar, this switch can be very useful in lowering falsely emphasized bass frequencies that can ruin a track.

Microphone Setup Options and Considerations

When available in a particular microphone, one may employ various recording possibilities by switching among directional patterns.

Pad Switch

Some microphones have a *pad switch* to reduce microphone sensitivity (normally by about –10 dB) when a signal level is too high.

Low-Cut Switch

This switch involves strong signal attenuation to reduce bass at 60, 80, 100, or 120 Hz, depending on the mic design.

Shock Mounts

A *shock mount* is a special mount that elastically suspends the microphone in a rigid frame to reduce random noise pickup, especially noise transmitted from the floor to the mic stand.

Phantom Power

This involves an electrical source of 48 volts made available from the preamp or mixing console through the same balanced microphone cable that carries the audio signal. Some condensers also offer battery-powered operation. Tube condenser mics almost always require a special power supply to deliver adequate power to the tube. In most cases, one must not supply these microphones with (extra) phantom power.

Maximum Sound Pressure Level (SPL)

This value (given in decibels, dB) is the maximum volume level that a microphone can tolerate without generating audible distortion. Most dynamic microphones are very resilient and can function in extremely high SPL situations. In comparison, condenser microphones are usually much more sensitive than dynamics, and thus have a much lower maximum SPL.

Self-Noise Level

This is the measurement of how much inherent noise is produced by the microphone. The lower this value, of course, the less such noise is likely to appear in the quiet moments of a recording. Condenser microphones typically have lower self-noise levels than dynamics.

Impulse Response

This is the ability of a microphone to respond to and accurately pass on strong transients without causing distortion.

Basic Types of Microphones

Dynamic Microphones

Generally, *dynamic microphones* are characterized by their relatively low price and robust, damage-resistant construction. They perform with aplomb in high sound pressure level (SPL) environments without creating distortion. They operate somewhat like loudspeakers in reverse, with a magnet and electric coil (or, in certain cases, a ribbon), in which movement of an element induces an electric current.

Moving Coil Microphones

This kind of dynamic microphone capsule employs a suspended membrane, which is connected to an induction coil in a magnetic field. When the membrane is moved by air, the motion creates an induced electric current reflecting the audio wave, and thus vaguely corresponds to the idea of a "reverse speaker." Although microphones of this design are extremely durable, creating a very linear response with them is difficult to the point of being impractical.

Ribbon Microphones

This design employs an extremely fine aluminum strip suspended between the poles of powerful permanent magnets. Air motion produces enough movement in the ribbon to generate a very refined signal, with impulse and linear frequency response comparable to (but sonically different from) first-rate condenser microphones. Most ribbon mics lack condenser-type "head amps" and thus need exceptional preamplifiers. Ribbon mics are also unusually sensitive and subject to damage from sudden movement or abuse from excessive SPL sources.

Condenser Microphones

This design consists of a very thin, generally gold-plated membrane mounted in close proximity to a charged metal plate, which in effect creates the electrical "condenser." This membrane responds to air movement that modifies the distance between it and the charged backplate, which in turn modifies the circuit capacitance and, with it, the electrical charge that finally becomes the audio signal. Most condensers need an external power source (or phantom power) and, compared to the majority of dynamic mics, have very good impulse response. Moreover, their frequency response is very linear and they have very high sensitivity.

Electret Microphones

These microphones are sometimes erroneously referred to as condensers because their construction is so similar. The critical difference is that electrets have a permanently magnetized backplate (with a typical life of perhaps 20 years) instead of the phantom-powered electrical magnet of true condensers. This

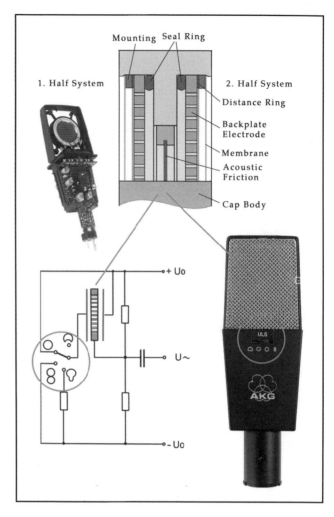

microphone type is often produced in large quantities by better microphone companies. Models may reach the sonic quality of first-rate condensers, and their built-in head amps are often suited for situations where only optional battery power may be available. This makes them an excellent choice for outdoor recording situations where phantom power might not be possible. As with condensers, electret mics have much higher output than typical dynamics, making them generally superior for low SPL situations. For recording devices that have no low-noise microphone inputs, electrets should definitely be preferred over dynamics. Of course, there is a limit with regard to high SPL sources. The electret microphone's technical SPL limits typically lie somewhere at our ear's threshold of pain (120 dB). So, if you're standing in an auto body shop next to a large sheet-metal press and have to scream into your interview partner's ear, it's also likely that your electret mic (and recording) will suffer from high SPL distortion.

Boundary Layer Microphones

This is a design (whose name is a registered trademark of Crown microphones) that focuses pickup on the wave buildup occurring near flat reflecting surfaces. The microphone incorporates a membrane that is bound flat to a larger plate that may be placed on the floor or wall. It typically has a "half-omni" directional characteristic and very smooth frequency response.

With more standard microphone designs, a problem may occur when a sound source and its floor reflections arrive at the mic at different times, which creates interference or cancellations—the so-called comb distortion effect. These lead to an ugly sound coloration—for example, nasality. As a first solution, one should move the microphone so that fewer room reflections and more sound from the source arrive at the mic. Another is the use of the boundary layer microphone, whose pickup design avoids such interference. With a unique or good room ambiance, however, the boundary layer mic can also serve as an excellent ambient pickup support microphone.

This sort of mix is optimal for being fixed to the surface of a grand piano cover, as a support microphone when recording bass drum tracks, live theater and concert recordings, and conference recordings.

Large Diaphragm and Tube Microphones

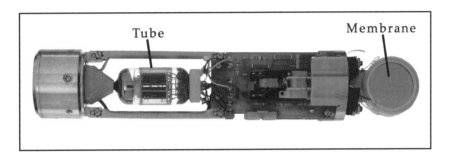

Large diaphragm microphones are those with membranes of a diameter of about 25 millimeters, compared to other "normal" condenser membrane sizes of roughly 10 to 25 millimeters. In general, smaller diaphragm microphones may exhibit a more detailed sound owing to their less massive diaphragm. A large diaphragm construction can typically produce a fuller low-range response. It's important to remember that choosing a microphone is often more about finding a particular sound than getting "perfect" signal reproduction.

Tube variations of the large diaphragm type are often the mics of choice because of their special "tube sound," which provides that certain presence through their initial built-in tube amplification stage.

Digital Microphones

These are, in effect, analog condenser microphones that have an integrated analog to digital converter for immediate transmission via digital cable in AES/EBU format. This makes a microphone pre-amp unnecessary, as the output may go directly to a digital mixing console. Depending on the manufacturer, these mics may also have extra features such as the ability to electronically save or "memorize" directional characteristics, pad and bass roll-off, and other settings. They can provide the user with the ability to control the microphones using remote-control software—meaning, of course, that the engineer has constant, centralized mic control during a studio session. In addition, the mic type and serial number may be digitally registered in the mic along with electronic warning and ready light information.

Taking Precautions Against High Sound Pressure Levels

In principle, very loud signals (caused by trombones, trumpets, and high impulse level drums) are less likely to damage dynamic (i.e., non-ribbon) microphones due to their robust construction and modus operandi. One must, however, be very careful to protect condensers. Although condensers have a wider frequency response, they often are more susceptible to high SPL distortion.

When your recording situation involves very loud signal levels, you should consider using a good dynamic mic, or at least employing the condenser pad switch, although the latter can lead to bandwidth limitations. Without either of these precautions, a microphone overdriven by sound levels that are too high runs the risk of causing an even less attractive alternative: distortion.

Stereo Microphone Techniques

There are two basic stereo recording techniques: *time-based* and *intensity-based*.

Time-Based Stereo Recording

This type of stereo recording technique relies upon creating a stereo image as a result of the difference in time of a signal's arrival between two microphones. Also referred to as *phase-based stereo*, this system helps to ensure outstanding bass response. The human ear can assemble a stereo image based on differences between times of signal arrival. Mono compatibility, however, is not particularly good with this configuration. Nowadays, despite this difficulty, time-based stereo recording still figures prominently, even in cases where a recording might be planned for mono radio broadcasts.

A-B Microphone Setup

This type of setup requires microphones with identical characteristics, though the pickup patterns chosen may themselves be varied to accommodate specific recording situations. For example, when working with an orchestra, omni-patterned microphones tend to create a recording in which the signal level differences between the stereo pair are minimal. With directional microphones, such as cardioid or hypercardioid, such differences will be more pronounced. If one wishes to have such a difference, it is only necessary to rotate the mics so that the capsules point slightly more towards each other to increase this effect—but without narrowing the stereo pattern appreciably.

Intensity-Based Stereo Recording

Intensity-based stereo involves recording only the level differences between what will be two stereo channels. To achieve this end, one places two microphones closely together so that no phase/time differences occur between the two capsules.

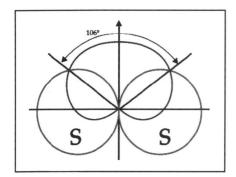

M-S Microphone Setup

In this configuration, a microphone with the chosen pattern is mounted facing the sound source and is referred to as the middle (M) component. A second microphone, referred to as the side (S) component, is set to a figure-eight pattern and is placed with its two figure-eight lobes at a 90-degree left/right angle to the middle microphone.

The stereo image is not a direct result of microphone placement, but rather of a sum and difference in the combined middle and side microphone components—the result of splitting the figure-eight signal, inverting one of the separated signals, and mixing all of them together.

- Left channel: M + S
- Right channel: M + S

X-Y Microphone Setup

This configuration requires two microphones of the same pattern. In most cases, this means the use of a cardioid pattern. The microphones should be positioned with their capsules crossing one above the other on a central axis. When precisely placed, the arriving sound waves meet both capsules at the same moment in time. When properly done, this assures an error-free stereo image.

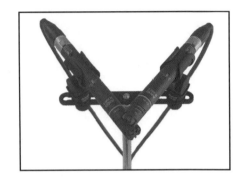

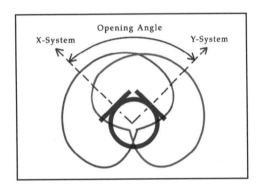

The stereo field is determined by the area within the angle of the two crossed microphones, as measured between the capsules. Increasing this angle increases the width of the recorded field. This setup provides a pick-up angle between 135 and 180 degrees and creates excellent stereo images of orchestral and wind ensembles. It is also mono compatible.

ORTF Setup

This system—named for the Office de Radiodiffusion Télévision Française, which developed the technique—is in fact a mixture of stereo recording approaches in which both intensity and time-based stereo are employed. It is designed to emulate the way human hearing works. Microphones are spaced at a distance comparable to that of a pair of adult human ears. With the microphones placed about 17 centimeters apart and directed at an angle of approximately 180 degrees, this setup can deliver a very natural sonic image. Larger separation is possible to create a wider (i.e., "stronger") stereo image. The sonic quality of this configuration lies somewhere between the X-Y and A-B microphone techniques.

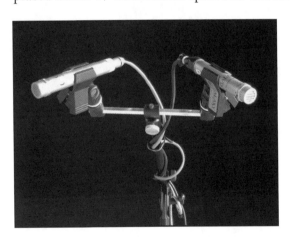

This stereo recording setup is almost exclusively achieved through two small-diaphragm cardioid microphones. An effective means for ORTF is a permanently installed mount or a dedicated microphone system.

Bass Drums

Introduction

Here, the prerequisites for a good recording are, of course, high quality drums and a drummer who knows exactly how to tune them.

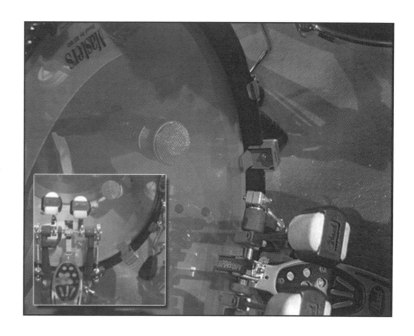

A bass drum is most often recorded with two microphones, one inside the bass for "kick," and a second outside—placed in front of the drum's resonator—to record instrument presence. Both microphones working together produce the most natural sound, since when one stands before the drum, one hears equally the "kick" from the skin as well as the instrument "presence."

Of course, when one has the means and an adequate number of free mixer channels, one may benefit from recording the bass drum with three or even four mics, as this may ensure valuable additional sonic variety. Often, as an extra measure of security, a trigger microphone (in conjunction with a drum module) may be added to fix any weak attacks that may show up during mixing.

How to Capture "Kick"

An engineer captures the so-called quality of bass drum "kick" by placing a microphone inside the drum. This requires cutting a 30- to 40-centimeter hole in the resonator skin so that the microphone (or stand) can be properly positioned within. The mic is best placed in the bass drum some 10 to 20 centimeters from the middle of the skin, pointing toward the area where the instrument skin is hit.

This kind of placement creates a very strong "kick" sound because the direct impulse of the drumstick is recorded. When the microphone is placed in the bass drum away from the skin, one hears an increase in fullness of sound due to the added presence of interior drum reflections. As desired drum quality can vary from song to song, it is recommended that the engineer try various mic positions to achieve the desired results.

Moreover, some recording producers want to have more of a direct "kick" while others would rather mix a song with a more voluminous sound. One should never underestimate the importance of the bass drum in a recording, especially in modern music, where the sonic effects of rhythm may be the most important ingredients.

How to Capture "Presence"

In order to get the right amount of presence, the microphone should be placed some 20 to 30 centimeters from—and pointing toward the middle of—the sound hole. In this way, the mic may best pick up the sound that is projected out into the room via the small sound hole. To understand the logic of recording in this location, one need only sit before the performing drummer and listen—but please be sure to use hearing protection.

The Use of Insulating Material in Bass Drums

It is possible to improve the sound of less-than-perfect drums by adding insulating material, such as a cover. However, one often forgets that this kind of alteration can completely eradicate the particular sonic quality of the instrument's wood, as envisioned by its designer. It's not uncommon for drummers to waltz into a music shop, buy a drum set based on the quality of the bass sounds, and then stuff it full of sound-destructive insulation—something that some of us can't, for the life of us, understand! Or, too often, the sound engineer focuses only on the big sound of the bass drum and nothing else. But one should never forget that a recording you make today will sound the same 30 years from now. Once it's done, it's done, so do it right!

Microphone Recommendations

• Inside: Condenser or high-quality dynamic microphones.

• Outside: Condenser (including tube mic) or high-quality dynamic microphones (cardioid pattern).

Snare Drums

The snare drum is very different sonically from the bass drum. Sounds are produced by the kettle and the skin and, depending on the size of these, will contain varying degrees of high or low frequencies. In addition, the snares themselves can be very loud.

I recommend recording the snare drum with two microphones: one focused on picking up the immediate fall of the sticks, and the second to pick up the sonic quality created by the instrument's tension, which is influenced substantially by the snares. In a mix, the snares may comprise a large part of the overall sonic effect. The recording microphone should be 3 to 10 centimeters from the skin, and it can point to either the instrument middle or brim. One should also consider positioning the snare microphone so as to include the hi-hat cymbals in the same angle, thereby reducing undesirable and irritating bleed-through or cross-talk of the hi-hats into the snare microphone.

In recording the snares themselves, one should place the microphone about 10 to 20 centimeters from—and to the side of—the resonator skin, pointing it toward the resonator middle.

Microphone Recommendations

• Condenser or high-quality dynamic microphones (cardioid pattern).

Hi-Hats

Place the microphone at a distance of about 5 to 10 centimeters from the hi-hat, and generally pointed toward the raised cymbal's center point; take care not to let the microphone touch the instrument. It is important to avoid directing the microphone toward the space between the hi-hat cymbals, as they create a strong air pressure wave as they meet—which is something you do not want to capture in a recording.

The microphone should be positioned to record as little of the snare drum sound as possible. Optimally, the mic should be 180 degrees from the snare itself so as to minimize the snare signal.

Microphone Recommendations

• Condenser microphones (cardioid pattern).

Toms

Before one even begins to record, it is extremely important to make sure that the toms are tuned properly. It is also advisable to consider having one microphone for each tom, which may call for independent mic stands and some good shock mounts.

With a good multi-pattern mic that offers a figure-eight pattern, one can record two toms with a single mic by placing it about 15 centimeters above and between the two toms.

Microphone Recommendations

- Condenser or high-quality dynamic microphones (cardioid pattern).

Ride Cymbals

Ride cymbals are best recorded with a cardioid condenser microphone directed at the bell from a distance of about 10 to 15 centimeters. If one wishes to have more sound from the bell, the microphone can be placed even closer; a greater distance will result in a track with a more "all-inclusive" instrument sound. Often, the only needed microphones in a room with good acoustics are the overheads.

Since ride cymbals have a large resonator, a strongly hit note may result in continuing resonance that causes undesirable effects. It is advisable to record at a lower level when sound from the bell is less of a consideration. Even at a reduced level, ride cymbals can contribute a great deal to the overall sound of a drum set. Therefore, as always, if you have any extra microphones and tracks, record a separate ride cymbal track, since this can have a special contributing impact on the entire mix—and, if not, it is an easy matter to erase the track.

Microphone Recommendations

- Condenser microphones (cardioid pattern).

Recording the Full Kit from Above

Overhead microphones are among the most important in drum recording because they capture the sound of the entire set. Without them, a drum recording will lack proper ambient acoustics, which add greatly to the clarity and reality of the sound.

The spatial richness in the "overhead" sound derives from the time delay between the overheads and the direct mics near individual drum instruments. That is, the sound reaches the direct mics sooner than those placed some 2 meters distant (i.e., the overheads). This time difference adds an important element to the recording.

In overhead recording, various stereo microphone placement systems are feasible. Among these are M-S, X-Y, and A-B setups. Another option when you have good room acoustics is to place additional microphones a number of meters away, and thus record tracks consisting predominantly of room ambiance. This adds a stunningly convincing quality to the mix.

In cases where room acoustics are exceptional, it is possible to leave the direct tom and snare microphones out entirely and rely only upon the overheads with a slight amount of the direct bass drum mic track mixed in.

Microphone Recommendations

- Overhead: Condenser microphones (cardioid pattern).

- Ambient: Condenser microphones (omni or cardioid pattern).

RECORDING VOCALS

The Basics

Because the microphone is the first link in the chain between the musician and the listener, a recordist should allow for the fewest possible compromises. This is important because no singer is going to appreciate being waltzed around the studio with tracks that fail because the wrong mic was used. What works is trying more than one mic in order to learn which one sounds good with which voice. The up-side is that it isn't always the most expensive mic that achieves the best track.

It is fairly standard procedure to employ large diaphragm condenser microphones for voices. Often, these are the best of the switching, multi-pattern variety. The omni and cardioid patterns in such mics often are the most advisable. It also makes sense to place such a mic in a good shock mount, which will assist in neutralizing any extraneous noises the singer may make, such as foot vibrations.

Pop Screens

Words that have strong "p" or "t" sounds can wreak havoc with a singer's tracks when they are over a certain level. It is possible to use a standard windscreen that comes with many microphones, but higher levels really require a specially designed screen. With it, fewer highs are lost and the singer can stay as close to the mic as she or he wishes without the danger of causing problems.

Backing Vocals

In backing vocals there should always be at least one microphone per singer. The use of mobile dividers will help with proper performer isolation. Differences in the levels of each singer can and should be watched for adjustment, even with—or perhaps because of—the differing EQ, processing, etc. of each voice. The room and number of different background voices will help to determine whether to use a mic with a cardioid or omni pattern.

Performer Monitoring

The singer most definitely needs a good headphone mix to be able to follow what is happening in the mix. Such a mix also serves as a "motivating" element for the singer. Most singers also prefer a touch of echo or reverb in such a mix in order to maintain an authentic feeling for what the voice will sound like—how it will "sit"—in the final mix.

Choosing Headphones

The best choice for proper isolation in such recording situations is a so-called "enclosed" or circumaural design so that, for example, during playback none of the headphone signal bleeds through into a singer's closely placed microphone.

The Recording Session

- Give the singer a chance to warm up with playback. This also allows time for the engineer to adjust the headphone mix and make mic adjustments.

- Only when the singer is satisfied with these warm-up playbacks is it then reasonable to begin laying down tracks.

- First, try a run-through of a complete song as orientation for both singer and engineer. This will also help to determine how prepared the singer is relative to the kind of recording session that will take place, and what recording procedures may be used. One can either record a number of complete takes and use the best parts to create the final complete song, or work from section to section (e.g., verse to verse) and do multiple takes of each. The latter method often gives one more overall control, since one gets a better view by dealing with shorter, individual sections one at a time.

Tips

- Use a pop screen.

- When available, use the microphone's low-cut switch.

- Choose the correct mic pattern.

- Use a good shock mount.

Microphone Recommendations

- Large diaphragm condenser microphones (omni or cardioid pattern).

RECORDING ELECTRIC BASSES

The Basics

There are basically two possibilities when recording an electric bass.

1. Route the instrument output directly from the bass pickup to the mixing console (or to the mixer via the preamp)

2. Record via microphones from the bass amp/speaker ensemble (so-called *cabinet miking*), which creates a recording that is truer to the bassist's performed sound

Recording Amplified Sound

Position the microphone approximately 10–30 centimeters to the side of the speaker. Depending on performer preferences, one can increase the master speaker volume level to capture more sound.

To record a "pure amplifier sound," the best option is to route the sound directly from the amp's "line out," "record out," or "direct out" over a direct injection (DI) box to the mixer. This is the most common procedure. The DI box need only be used with a "passive" bass, since an "active" bass can cause very high output levels that generally preclude the need for a DI unit. When recording with a band, it makes the most sense not to use a mic, but instead to route the bass signal directly from its amplifier to the mixer. This way, the player can follow his or her track on headphones without interference from other players that a mic may pick up, while still maintaining a clean signal.

An alternative is to mix the direct amplifier signal with that of the speaker, something that also may add to the signal level. It is in any case advisable to experiment with various microphones in search of the best sound. Ideal distances from microphones vary from 2 centimeters to just over 1 meter, but bear in mind that "room" recordings with electric bass do not usually amount to much.

Recording Direct Signal

This approach entails routing the bass signal directly through a high quality preamp, adding compression, and then sending it to the mixer or hard disk recorder.

The bass sound is often compressed during a recording session, and the engineer must develop a sense for whether there is enough desired string noise or "dirt" coming through; this is generally a question of taste. One should not attempt to eliminate an individual string's sound quality, however, as it may later be missed in the mix as a "true sound" component that helps identify the bass in the midst of other instruments.

Microphone Recommendations

- Amplifier (cabinet) recording: Condenser or high quality dynamic microphones (cardioid pattern).

RECORDING ACOUSTIC GUITARS

The Basics

When recording an acoustic guitar, one normally looks to get the best signal from directly in front of the sound hole, where the harmonic fundamentals are most present and thereby provide the most convincing sound properties available from the instrument's wood-based construction. In cases where a sound richer in overtones or perhaps even an increased presence of finger-on-string noise is sought, an added microphone may be directed toward the nut. In this situation, one may choose to add a small-diaphragm mic, which provides a more brilliant result. On the other hand, using a large-diaphragm microphone may provide a fuller sounding track. Microphone distance is generally 20–50 centimeters. If one manages to obtain a recording room with very good acoustics, it is then possible to enhance this instrument's recorded sound with a boundary layer microphone, which is particularly suited for this kind of recording. This mic should be placed on the floor about 1.5 meters from the player, and the result mixed with the close mic.

Guitars with Pickups

Many guitarists possess an acoustic instrument with a built-in pickup. This, however, is normally not ideal for recording because the sound lacks the proper resonance and fullness. Such internal mics may have their uses, but not in serious recording, where they tend to provide a sound limited strongly to the instrument's mid-range.

Recording Tips

A very effective guitar recording technique is to record guitar takes with two very different microphones and then combine both of them in the mix. This often leads to a much more "genuine" final mix—one that captures the instrument's character much better than a single mic.

RECORDING ELECTRIC GUITARS

Recording Amplifiers

A good way to manage the recording of an electric guitar amplifier is with one or more of the following microphone arrangements.

- Employ two microphones (i.e., cabinet miking), one for direct sound some 5–10 centimeters away and at the edge of the speakers being fed by the guitar amp, and a second microphone some 3–4 meters away pointing to the upper rim of the speaker (so that with this mic you also record room acoustics).

- When room acoustics are especially good, more ambient mics may be used. Place two microphones as a stereo pair some 3–5 meters away, or so that one is about 6 meters away and directed at the upper edge of the amplifier.

- Place two condenser microphones at approximately the middle of the speaker cone, but also somewhat to the side so that that sound waves are not transmitted too directly into the microphone capsules (the sound pressure can overdrive the mics and create an ugly, "boomy" track). The height of the microphones should be horizontal and directed toward the speaker middle, about halfway between the speaker's center and edge. Condenser mics may be 2–3 centimeters away from the speaker grill cloth, with dynamic mics even closer. Find the best position through simple trial and error with each different amp/speaker combination.

It is highly recommended to record guitar amp/speaker setups with multiple microphones and then later, when mixing, to decide on the best combination of those mics to produce your personal mix of direct and room acoustics.

The microphone selection should also be based upon guitar amp output power and whether a very clean or distorted sound is desired. In such cases it is worth it to try out a number of microphone combinations. Of course, there is also the option of bypassing the amp/speaker through direct (i.e., pickup) recording and/or through "amp simulation" to the console or as a console insert. In laying down pre-production room tracks, record using the highest quality amplifier. Such an amp lends the guitar adequate bass presence and analog warmth that one cannot get in simulations. This equipment selection also assures the correct tracking of a guitarist's own characteristic, authentic sound.

Microphone Recommendations

- Large diaphragm condenser microphones (cardioid pattern).

- High-grade dynamic microphones (cardioid pattern).

RECORDING PIANOS

If the correct instrumental and room acoustics are available, there is nothing quite like a beautiful piano recording. Whenever the piano is given a supportive role in a song—for example, in a ballad—it pays to take the trouble to employ less expensive samples (i.e., MIDI).

Microphone Techniques

Depending on the size of the grand piano, one usually records this instrument with two or three microphones, combining these for the desired sound.

In pop and jazz recordings, the mics are often directed toward the hammers in order to capture their harder and more direct impact.

One can achieve a larger dynamic range through the placement of additional microphones directed at a distance of about 10–40 centimeters from the sound holes and toward the soundboard. This placement adds room ambiance. The bass range is best recorded by positioning microphones near the string tuners at a distance of about a meter.

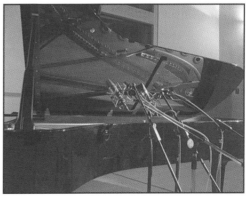

Microphone Setup According to Straus-Paket

Of course, one can make a stereo recording with just two microphones. Another system—called *Straus-Paket* after its German founder—utilizes a combination of omni and cardioid microphones bound together, one on top of the other, whose combined signal results in a variable, "wide-cardioid" pattern. This setup therefore needs four microphones. To best avoid phase problems, have these two microphone capsules located at precisely the same point. This placement also results in

what is in essence a "vertical stereo" image. The upper stereo pair may be mixed toward their omni-patterns (with a greater room component), and the lower pair toward cardioid patterns, producing a more focused stereo, or vice versa. With both of these configurations, one can adjust the final mix to taste. Although a grand piano's sound emanates more strongly in the horizontal plane, high-frequency projection is not the main problem. Therefore, the two microphones are vertically rather than horizontally placed.

Classical Recording

To ensure that the piano's entire sound spectrum is being recorded, it is advisable that both microphone pairs be placed in the middle area of the piano frame at a slightly farther distance. One should look for a location where the entire frequency range is most in balance. In classical recording, the microphone of choice is often one that has a very natural, transparent quality with very little coloring.

Pop Recording

In the pop recording field, a piano's attack is more important than in classical recording. Therefore, microphones may be placed further into the instrument. This is naturally dependent on aesthetic considerations for the song. With such a placement there is less lid reflection and thus more direct string sound. The angle between the paired microphones should be somewhat larger in order to improve the stereo image and maintain a better balance between the lows and highs.

Grand Piano Plus Orchestra

When recording with an orchestra, it is advisable to raise the piano lid only to the minimum level so as to avoid bleed-through from other instruments. The piano lid opening should not be directed toward the orchestra, as this will cause later mix-down problems with extraneous external instrumental sounds, and with maintaining the piano's individual sonic character. If the piano must remain completely closed, one can employ a pressure boundary microphone inside the piano's frame.

Upright Pianos

In recording an upright piano, it is recommended to leave the upper instrument lid open. One should direct a stereo pair of condenser microphones from above downwards towards the strings. Removing the front cover can also lend more openness and room presence to the sound.

Microphone Recommendations

• Condenser microphones (cardioid pattern).

The Basics

The original "Leslie sound" consisted of a speaker cabinet containing a fixed downward-directed bass woofer, and a second mid-upper–range speaker pointing into a rotating air canal or wave guide that directed these mid-upper frequencies up through a rotating set of horns to, in effect, produce vibrato. Typically, three microphones are used to record this sound: one for the bass and the others for the two separate (right/left) cabinet sound holes through which the rotating horn sounds emanate. Should the Leslie ensemble consist of a single, full-range loudspeaker, one may place the two microphones on opposite corners of the rotating horn assembly—something that also provides a wide stereo image.

Microphone Recommendations

* Condenser microphones (all in cardioid pattern) or, depending on personal preference, an omni for the lower frequencies.

RECORDING SAXOPHONES

The Basics

Recording a saxophone is a simpler process than with many other instruments. One should keep in mind, however, that its sound radiates more from the area around the keys than from the bell. Usually, the best results are obtained from a cardioid microphone placed about 30–50 centimeters from, and directed toward, the keys. But the nearer one comes to the keys, the more one will also find key and air noises in the recorded track. Moreover, it is important to watch out for large movements by the player—these should be restricted to the microphone's optimal recording radius.

Another way of solving this problem is to use microphones that can attach to the instrument. These, however, produce a sound that is not as desirable, due in part to the lack of fullness from the smaller microphone and its diaphragm size.

Microphone Recommendations

• Condenser microphones (cardioid pattern).

• When recording a wind ensemble or a saxophonist with a more aggressive style, a good dynamic microphone can produce favorable results.

RECORDING FLUTES

The Basics

When recording a flute, it is important to keep in mind that it has a high degree of air noise, something that is usually not desired. When close miking is necessary due to space constraints, position the microphone 20–40 centimeters away and pointed down toward the player's mouth. A distance of 50–60 centimeters will lessen wind noise. A better approach is to use two microphones, the second of which may be placed some 40 centimeters to the player's side; this will also add more room presence.

Microphone Recommendations

* Condenser microphones (cardioid pattern).

The Basics

A clarinet projects both from its bell and its keys. It can produce a more brilliant tone when floor reflections are strong and the microphone is placed at a good distance from, and directed toward, its conical end piece. Placing the microphone slightly to one side can reduce key noise.

Microphone Recommendations

•   Condenser microphones (cardioid pattern).

RECORDING TRUMPETS, TROMBONES, AND FLUGELHORNS

The Basics

These instruments create extremely high sound pressure levels reaching up to 130 dB, which is enough to damage microphones not constructed for such levels. Therefore, consider employing good dynamic microphones placed at a distance of about 40 centimeters from the instrument bell.

For pop, jazz, and big band recordings, microphones should not be positioned directly in front of the bell, owing to the potential for microphone damage and varied levels (including the risk of distortion) due to player movement. Whenever possible, a microphone should be positioned to one side of the instrument.

When recording a larger wind ensemble or band, keep in mind that a single instrument track may be blemished from excessive bleed-through of other instruments—something that can be minimized by closer miking.

Microphone Recommendations

- Good dynamic microphones (cardioid pattern).

- Condenser microphones (cardioid pattern).

- Tube microphones (cardioid pattern).

Solo Pop Music Recording

One or two dynamic (cardioid) microphones about two meters away and in front of a horn serve well here, though a large diaphragm microphone may provide better low-frequency response. To enhance the recording of both indirect and direct sound, two additional dynamic (cardioid) microphones may be added behind the horn player and directed at the bell; this can be varied according to performer and engineer preference and to avoid excessive diffuse field sound. The rear microphones contribute to a robust horn sound that in pop music is important in maintaining the instrument's presence and in avoiding a covered horn sound.

Classical Recording

When recording classical music, the preference is for the most natural sound possible. This is best achieved through a spot microphone behind the player or, even better, one or two microphones at quite a distance from the player. Large-diaphragm microphones are often preferable over small.

Microphone Recommendations

• Dynamic, large-diaphragm (cardioid) microphones.

Recording Violins and Violas

The Basics

Because of the way in which these instruments are held—with the soundboard towards the ceiling—their sound also projects forcefully in that same direction. Microphone placement should take this into consideration.

A good condenser mic should be used. Its placement should be at least a half meter away from the instrument, unless one wishes for some reason to add considerable bow noise to the recording.

In particularly good room acoustics, one might consider the use of an omni-pattern mic. Otherwise, a cardioid-pattern mic may be best.

Microphone Recommendations

*   Condenser microphones (cardioid or omni pattern).

Recording Cellos and Contrabasses

Solo Recording

For all its size, the contrabass is an instrument that produces a limited signal level. For such a special case, it is very much up to the microphone to produce a good recording. In solo recording situations, a large diaphragm microphone is ideal and may be best placed in the area below the instrument's F-hole at a distance of about a foot. Experimenting with this distance will provide a tonal balance between lows and mids. For added string sounds, use a small condenser microphone attached to the bridge.

Ensemble Recording

In ensemble sessions, the lighter sound level of the contrabass creates the likelihood of bleed-through from other instruments. Often this can be countered by using a hypercardioid microphone in close proximity to the contrabass. If this sound is not satisfactory, another possibility is to use a built-in pickup. However, it is important to be aware of the tradeoff of the harsher pickup sound for the added volume or isolation it provides.

Microphone Recommendations

*   Condenser microphones ("kidney" or supercardioid pattern).

MICROPHONE PREAMPLIFIERS

A microphone preamplifier is responsible for raising the normally very low signal level of a microphone to a level high enough for use with a mixer or other devices. This can require up to a 2000-fold gain factor, which with other considerations provides for a market of disparate machine quality levels and prices. One might consider a preamp that corresponds to the quality of the microphone used, since later track quality is only as good as its original recorded signal. Preamps are available either built into mixing consoles or as single-purpose, outboard machines.

Parameters

- *Gain* regulates the input volume.

- *Output* regulates the output volume.

- *Tube gain* (if available) regulates the amount of gain that the tubes provide.

- A *hi-pass (rumble) filter* reduces undesirable low frequencies such as stage rumble or impulse noises (mostly between 50 and 80 Hz).

- *Phantom power* is the standard, required electrical power for condenser microphones, without which such microphones cannot function. Phantom power is standardized to 48 volts and is supplied via the microphone cable.

- A *phase inversion switch* inverts the phase of a channel.

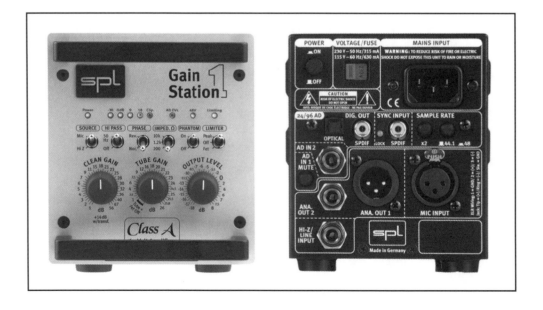

Levels

An engineer's attention to correct preamplifier level adjustment is of special importance. Initial signal levels must be set to avoid peak distortion, but not so low that noise levels become a problem.

A Tip for Using Phase Inversion

Though switching the *phase* (polarity) of a microphone is normally irrelevant in the final recording, it can be of great importance to, say, a singer during a session. When a singer is monitoring his or her performance via headphones, she or he hears the mix of this signal with actual head tones. The ability to reverse the phase of headphone signals can alleviate problems from this phenomenon, possible cabling errors, or phase inversion from multiple microphone sources.

ANALOG-TO-DIGITAL AND DIGITAL-TO-ANALOG CONVERSION

Analog to Digital (A/D) Conversion

In order to process an analog signal (from, say, a microphone) digitally, it is first necessary to convert the analog format to a digital one. To do this, an essentially fluid analog waveform is divided into individual segments based on small time divisions.

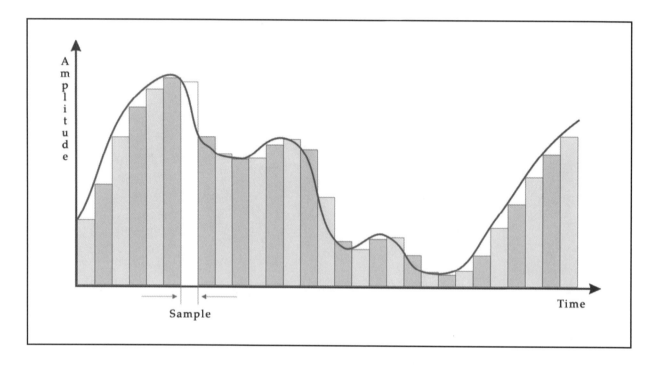

Word Bit Depth

The wave's amplitude defines a so-called *digital word*. In CD format, the *word depth* consists of 2^{16}, or 65,536 different values.

Because the quantization level stops at 0 dB, any value above this creates unacceptable *brick-wall clipping* and distortion. Such values must be "watched like a hawk" to ensure that none of this mathematically absolute and sonically unacceptable clipping occurs.

In stark contrast to this absolute limit is that of analog recording, where instead of a 0 dB absolute, one is granted a bit more leeway, allowing the input signal level to extend beyond theoretical (digital) limits and, in effect, offering expanded *headroom* that eases certain aspects of recording an available signal. In response to this problem, digital systems have increased the bit depth to 24 (2^{24}, or about 16.8 million) discrete samples. These added bits help to minimize the problem and create a greater sampling rate, although there is in reality no more headroom than before. The result is a qualitatively better digital signal with a much higher dynamic range. From the standpoint of converters—on purely physical grounds—higher resolution than this would not be sensible, as such an increase would produce no appreciable improvement in signal quality.

Quantization

This is the process whereby a waveform is "frozen" for a brief moment in time to, in effect, take a mathematical picture of the amplitude. Such a procedure includes very slight deviations between the actual and recorded values, which are known collectively as *quantization noise*. This noise is considerably lower with 24-bit resolution than with 16-bit, and although the difference is generally blanketed by the much higher-level audio signal, it may be noticeable in very quiet musical passages.

Sample Rate in kHz

This term defines the sampling frequency, and specifies how often per second a signal is assessed in time—for example, 44.1 kHz means 44100 times in one second. The greater this value, the more precisely we can arrive at a rate approximating true analog values and sonic quality. But this also puts a great deal of strain on a digital processor's computing power and adds enormously to the volume of data, which means large increases in required hard drive space and the need to adapt computing algorithms to such higher values.

Dithering

This is the technical process whereby quantization noise may be made less obtrusive. Quantization problems are most noticeable in quiet passages because the signal itself is represented by a fraction of the available word bit-depth: The lower a passage's amplitude, the fewer bits there are available to depict it. Dithering enters into the picture—in CD mastering, for example—by calculating a reduction of a 24-bit project to a 16-bit CD format, rounding off the values of bits 17–24 instead of simply truncating them.

Jitter

Jitter is the term used to describe unwanted noise and phase shifts that are caused when inaccurate clocking is used to define a digital moment. Too much jitter can lead to cumulative errors such as degraded stereo imaging, lower signal dynamic range, and, in extreme cases, audible distortion. The preemptive solution is high-quality clocking.

Digital to Analog (D/A) Conversion

Simply put, this refers to the conversion of a digital signal into an analog signal for routing to monitors or for processing in, for example, external analog effects machines.

Digital Formats

SPDIF (Sony/Philips Digital Interface)

- Cable lengths of up to 100 meters are possible.

- There is a two-channel limit.

- The maximum sampling rate is 96 kHz.

- This format uses unbalanced (i.e., 75-ohm impedance) cables with RCA connectors, or an optical TOSLINK cable.

AES/EBU (Audio Engineering Society/European Broadcast Union)

- Cable lengths of up to 100 meters are possible.

- This format has a balanced signal path.

- There is a two-channel limit.

- The maximum sampling rate is 96 kHz.

- This format uses balanced (110-ohm impedance) cables with XLR connectors.

ADAT (Alesis Digital Audio Tape)

- This is an eight-channel format.

X Optical Data Transfer

- This is over what is known as an *ADAT light pipe*.

- This is a bi-directional format.

- The sampling rate is 48 kHz.

S/MUX

- This format possesses properties similar to the ADAT format.

- It enables transference at a 96-kHz sampling rate through the use of two 48-kHz ADAT channels.

MADI (Multi-Channel Audio Digital Interface)

- This provides up to 56 mono channels via a single optical or coaxial cable.

- The transfer rate is from 16- to 24-bit at 32 to 48 kHz.

TDIF (TASCAM Digital Interface)

- This format uses unbalanced cables with 25 pol. sub-D connectors.

- A cable length of up to 5 meters is possible.

- This format is bi-directional.

- This allows for eight input and output channels.

- The transfer rate is 24-bit at 96 kHz.

MIXING CONSOLES

The central element in a recording studio is the mixing console. Here is the juncture for all signal paths, which will be "mixed and matched" in tone color and level.

Analog Mixers

Analog mixers usually have a control or switch for every parameter. The following will familiarize you with the most important of these.

Pad Switch

This enables a fixed lowering of an incoming signal level to avoid channel level peaks.

Gain Control (Microphone Pre-Amp)

A signal that a microphone sends directly to the console is typically very limited. Therefore, it must be brought up to an adequate working strength (at this console input). Most mixers have a peak meter or light to indicate when such a signal has surpassed its useful level, something which—together with the preamp—helps provide maximum signal strength and minimal noise (i.e., an optimal *signal-to-noise ratio*) as well as adequate dynamic range.

Phantom Power (+48 Volt)

This switch controls (globally or individually) the needed power to the mixer channel microphone inputs so that the condenser mics may function properly.

Equalizer (EQ)

Depending upon the complexity of the mixing console, these appear in what is called a *fully-* or *half-parametric* design. They offer various kinds of cut and boost to lower, middle, and high frequencies.

Low-Cut (Hi-Pass Filter)

This switch engages steep signal attenuation below a certain frequency, typically beginning at 80 or 100 Hz.

Auxiliary Controls

Aux Sends

Each mixer channel typically has more than one such optional and separate path, each with a level control. These auxiliary paths allow the engineer to detour a portion of the channel signal through other paths—to a compressor, for example. Another common use for auxiliary paths is to create a so-called *monitor mix* to be used, for example, for singer or instrumentalist monitoring during warm-up.

Aux Return

This is a level-controlled input that allows a processed signal from the auxiliary out—for example, a reverbed or otherwise processed vocal—to be brought back into the mix. As with the sends, there are typically a number of these returns. One should, by the way, prevent these from being misused as extra input channels.

Pre/Post Switch

This determines whether an auxiliary send is routed before or after the channel fader (*pre-fader* or *post-fader*, respectively) to the auxiliary bus.

To keep a monitor mix independent of the main mix, one can engage the pre-fader switch (or routing) and be able to eliminate the channel's signal without affecting the monitor mix.

Solo Function

This switch preempts all main mix routing and sends one or more channels exclusively to the main mix.

Panning Control (Mono Channels) and Balance Control (Stereo Channels)

These controls position the signals in the mix corresponding to their recorded location. In a standard (stereo) mixer, the signal is controlled one-dimensionally (left to right). A surround mixer adds yet a second dimension (front to rear).

Group Switch

This switch routes a group of channels to a subgroup fader, thereby allowing an entire set of channels to be controlled at the same time. Depending upon the console design, there may be an option for this submix to be routed to a special group output and/or to the master fader.

Channel Faders

Each channel has this fader, with which the respective channel's signal level may be controlled.

Master Fader

This controls the console's output and is responsible for the final mix level.

Other Connections

Inserts

An *insert* interrupts the signal, making it possible to route the channel signal to an effects processor and return it to the main mix. Typical insert effects would be a compressor, gate, equalizer, distortion, or de-esser.

Any added circuitry in the signal path (including automatic controls) may mean signal quality loss in cases where the signal must run through the automation circuitry. In very expensive consoles, automation may be implemented through *discrete circuitry*, meaning that the faders are controlled with independent motors and switches via relays. In such designs there is no electronic automation directly in the audio signal path.

Digital Mixing Consoles

In function and design, digital consoles resemble their analog counterparts, with the exception of digital signal paths. If a signal is initially analog, it must be converted to digital—something that also applies to the use of analog processing during the mix. On returning to the mixer, the signal continues to be processed digitally. The features offered by such a mixer are highly dependent on the available processing power.

Depending on the manufacturer and design philosophy, a console may have the following features.

- Signal path (routing) that is freely configurable.

- A fully-parametric equalizer in each channel and in each band (bass, middle, highs).

- Internal dynamics processing (compressor, limiter, gate) for each channel.

- Internal effects (hall, delay, chorus, flanger) for each channel.

- Graphic depiction of routings, filter curves, VU meters, preset lists, etc. via TFT (thin film transistor) LCD displays.

- External mouse and keyboard.

- Automated setups (fader movement, EQ settings, routings) that may be saved.

Should I Use a Digital Mixer or an Analog Mixer?

This is the million-dollar question! Each has its advantages and disadvantages. Popular opinion has it that digital mixers are rather cold and sonically inferior compared to analog mixers. This, however, is not a universal truth. The sound of a mixer is determined by a number of many factors, such as the algorithms in the processing of the signal path, the quality of the components, the bandwidth, the sample rate of the digital signal, as well as the input and output converters. Above a certain price class, it is difficult to distinguish between mixes from an analog or a digital console.

The quality and features of a digital mixing console increase significantly with each improvement in algorithm and processor speed.

Advantages and Disadvantages of Digital Mixers

Headroom

With a large headroom of around 32 dB per channel, it is difficult to reach signal saturation or distortion in the signal path. A mix with many instruments and the resulting sonic density—i.e., as a result of this typical analog headroom—can make this type of console easier to manage.

Bandwidth

This is the frequency range of an audio signal (that is, the range between the lowest and highest frequencies) in which a mixer may effectively process the audio components. The human ear hears, in ideal circumstances, frequencies between 20 Hz and 20 kHz, but the bandwidth of a mixer is theoretically without limit. In most mixers this range is practically100 kHz, and in very expensive consoles it can be up to 150 kHz. In a digital mixer, one needs about 150 kHz bandwidth to achieve the necessary doubling of the sample rate. This means that a more direct comparison between analog and digital mixers could be significant when the digital counterpart could work at 384 kHz/24-bit. At this point, there is theoretically no difference in bandwidth.

Real-Time Processing

In an analog console, the entire mixing process—including the insertion of external processors—takes place in real time. There are neither *latency problems* (i.e., signal path time delays) that must be accounted for, nor must the input/output signals be converted (A/D or D/A) to achieve these external processing goals—either of which can result in loss of signal quality.

Digital Signal Processing Power

In the digital realm, every process, internal effect, and inserted external outboard processor makes it necessary for the engineer to keep track of every expenditure and resource.

Automation

With the exception of switching and faders, there is little to nothing that can be automated in the analog realm. One must photograph or otherwise record the adjustment in order to recall important session setups. Because of these limitations, one must approach and realize goals in an analog mix somewhat differently—for example, through alternate organizational procedures or external equipment.

Sample Rate

The higher the signal level that is processed, the nearer one comes to the original signal. At very high sample rates, equalization remains in phase throughout the entire duration of a signal's processing. As a result, EQ may be attained via surgical procedures in specific frequency ranges—something that may be achieved in analog mixers only through extremely expensive EQ circuitry.

Compactness

With digital mixers, switching circuitry can be much more compact and, thanks to software, many of the console functions can be graphically displayed on a monitor. In this way, digital mixers achieve a reduced footprint, although this may also mean that certain ergonomic aspects are not available (for example, there may not be a control or knob for certain functions).

Simply put, a *monitor*—and this includes headphones—converts electrical impulses into audible sound waves. Those used in a recording studio should have a true or *linear* reproduction capability (i.e., one which introduces little or no coloration), and should be chosen to match the playback room. The integration of monitors into a room is dependent upon the room having good ambience to begin with.

Good impulse response is just as important, if not more so, than linear frequency response. A good studio monitor delivers a transparent, neutral sound that is not to be compared with that coming from hi-fi speakers, as these are often designed with coloration to impress listeners with their "fuller" sound.

Impulse Response

This is the term used to describe certain physical properties of a speaker. A properly reproduced signal impulse means that no time or phase distortion occurs, indicating a precise, natural sound reproduction. A speaker's greatest challenge in signal reproduction is the accurate reproduction of such short impulses. Typically, the cleaner these are, the better the other characteristics (both long- and short-sustaining tones) will be.

An Example: Snare Drum Impulse

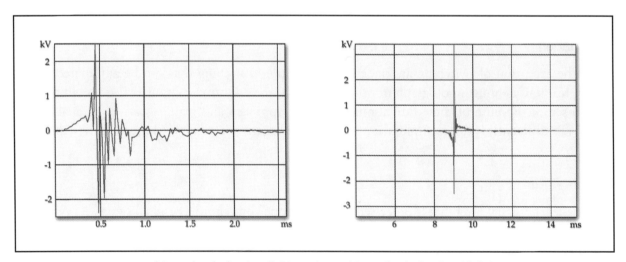

Bad impulse behavior (left) and good impulse behavior (right)

To portray this sound accurately, a speaker cone must move every bit as quickly as the snare skin. The speaker that responds more slowly than this and cannot replicate the snare motion is considered to have *bad impulse response*.

Latency Issues

There aren't any speakers that can reproduce a signal at 0 Hz. The typical effective monitor bass response begins between 20 and 40 Hz. A lower filter than this effective frequency is responsible for generating latency, usually of about 10 milliseconds for analog and 5 milliseconds for digital speakers.

Drivers

Speakers function through electrical signals that flow through an attached coil, in which there is a powerful magnet that reacts with and against the field. Together, the magnet and the coil drive the cone, which in turn reproduces the desired sound waves. The stronger the magnet, the more effectively and correctly these sound waves and impulses may be reproduced. This is the case not only with loud signals but with quiet ones as well.

Passive Monitors

A *passive* monitor requires a separate power amplifier. An amplifier may be constructed as a *two-way system*, which contains one speaker for the bass-mid range and another for the higher frequencies. It may have two contacts or posts for signal inputs, which may be fed by two separate mono power amps. An alternative is to employ two stereo power amps with the left output routed to the bass-mid range and the right output routed to the high range.

Advantages

*   Passive monitors are less expensive.

*   One can decide upon which power amp he or she wishes to use.

Disadvantages

*   It is more troublesome to optimize a passive system's sound quality. Often, individual components in the chain are not optimized, and one may also have to add large "design margin" increases (in amp output, cabling, etc.) to achieve the same results as with active systems, although the latter will be comparatively much more expensive.

Active Monitors

Active monitors have a clear advantage in that the integrated power amps are built into the enclosure and tuned to their speakers. Shorter resulting cable lengths decrease potential signal and sound quality loss. They are so well adapted to each other that speakers are protected from damage due to overdriving.

Analog Speakers

As the name implies (particularly in active types), this construction uses analog design and parts throughout.

Digital Speakers

These are active monitors that have a digital input (AES/EBU or SPDIF) that can be fed directly from a digital mixer's output. This results in the loss-free transmission of a signal, where it is then converted and amplified within the speaker itself. Typically, these monitors include software frequency correction to maintain a linear reproduction and to reach an optimal impulse response. Such speakers may also have an alternative analog input to work with mixers that have only this kind of output.

Problems with Loudness

In one scenario, a monitor is digitally connected to a mixer. Maximum loudness may occur when a signal contains full 16- or 24-bit resolution, depending on the working bitrate. At lower signal levels, the word depth is reduced, resulting in a decrease in signal quality—possibly, only 12 or even eight bits of a 24-bit signal may be present. To counter this, some manufacturers have introduced separate cable-connected monitor controls to allow maximum digital signal levels to be transmitted from a console. Adjustments to monitor volume are made after the signals have been converted to analog, thus helping to eliminate digital quality loss in cases where there would be limited bit resolution and quality from low-level musical passages.

Why Should I Use a Digital Monitor?

In recent years, more and more audio productions have worked increasingly in the digital domain. Often a signal is converted from analog to digital immediately after being recorded with a microphone, and it remains digital from then on. Such signals can, through a digital monitoring system, sustain a more loss-free processing chain.

In a two-way monitoring system, signals are divided between the high and mid-low speakers via a frequency-separating filter that can result in physical delay and time distortion. The filter can also result in phase shifts. For example, in the case of a snare drum—an instrument that has a wide frequency range—the reproduction of the different frequencies through the two-way system results in smearing the impulse on the time axis. In the case of a digital monitor, there can be a processor that mathematically adjusts various frequencies to a correct phase relation and thus passes on to the power amp a signal that achieves better impulse response and activates the monitor cone optimally.

Nearfield Monitors

These are speakers that work optimally at a listener distance of between 1 and 1.5 meters.

Advantages

- The recording engineer sits directly in the monitor sound field, which through short source separation minimizes unwanted influences from room acoustics.

- This design allows for less massive cones and faster reaction in the speaker mechanism, resulting in more easily attained and precise impulse responses than with larger monitors. Thus, the transmission of percussive sounds is improved.

Disadvantages

- The limited listening distance and sound field tends to create only one optimal hearing location, the so-called *sweet spot*.

- The generally limited size of such monitors requires a *subwoofer* in order to reproduce sounds below 50 or 60 Hz. This functions best when purchased in conjunction with the monitors.

- In typical nearfield seating, there may be a distance difference between the higher and lower frequencies. In such cases, help may be provided through coaxial monitors.

Farfield Monitors

These are monitors that are effective at a 3–5 meter distance. Most are much larger than nearfield monitors and are built into walls.

Advantages

- Their larger size and emission angle may provide ideal points for 2–4 listeners sitting at a mixing console.

- Farfield monitor size provides for more presence and loudness, so that special listening situations such as disco or dance productions may be more readily simulated.

Disadvantages

- Room reflections play a greater role in the listening experience. The room quality is therefore much more important.

- The greater the cone mass and throw, the greater the possibility for inaccuracies. There is a much greater chance for distortion.

Using a Subwoofer in the Studio

There are two basic categories.

* The mono subwoofer, which is added to a stereo pair responsible for mid-high frequencies.

* Subwoofers for each channel—a stereo pair, in other words—so that both mid- and low-frequency signals below a certain range are reproduced by these woofers.

Bass Management

Nowadays, professional studio setups provide for *5.1 surround sound*, which is comprised of five identical speakers along with a single subwoofer responsible only for the lowest frequencies of around 80–160Hz.

Bass management now comes into play, providing for routing an adjustable range of low frequencies from all five speakers to the bass subwoofer. This becomes especially important in the case of smaller satellite speakers more typical of consumer listening setups that are unable to reproduce lower frequencies. In such systems, there is an amplifier procedure to provide for increased, credible bass response.

Alternative Monitoring Options

Coaxial Monitors

This is a design in which the bass and high frequencies are placed in a common axis. Sound waves emanate from a point source—that is, from a single area of the speaker. The advantages of this are that in listening within a restricted distance, all of the frequencies follow essentially the same path to the ears and phase-shift problems are eliminated.

Headphones

Mixing with headphones—even with the best high-end models—is not recommended, because headphone sound properties are not linear, nor is there compensation for room acoustics. However, headphones can be useful for effects programming or listening for undesirable noises.

Monitor Positioning

* A proper distance from rear and side walls should be maintained. This will help to avoid standing waves, especially in bass frequencies. To accomplish this, they should be placed at least 60 centimeters away from each wall.

* Aim for symmetrical placement in the room.

- An optimal stereo listening spot occurs at the point of a 30-degree, equilateral triangle—the sweet spot.

- The two monitors should point exactly at the listener's head.

- Higher frequencies should radiate directly toward the ears.

- To avoid any sympathetic resonances, monitors should stand on separate mounts and not be integrated into sound-altering console furnishings or frames.

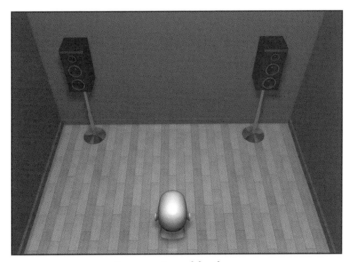

Incorrect positioning

Correct positioning

SOUND FORMATS

Mono

The very first recordings over 100 years ago were made strictly in mono. Today mono is also referred to as *single-channel playback*, a technique that is used most often now as an effect. Many established artists use it as a contrasting element to the now-standard stereo. There is no noticeable spaciousness in a mono playback, and from any point in the room mono sounds essentially the same as in any other.

Stereo

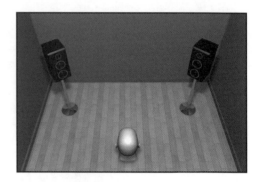

Over time, one-channel playback was gradually and logically expanded to two channels. This so-called *stereophonic sound* established itself towards then end of the 1950s, only about 20 years after it first appeared. This idea was the first attempt to evoke the spatial qualities of a room from intensity or time differences between the two recorded channels.

Nowadays, almost every playback or broadcast medium can transmit or play this stereo format. An optimal placement of the loudspeakers for stereo systems might look as follows. Loudspeakers should be placed in an equilateral triangle relative to the listener, who forms the third part of the triangle. At the ideal listening point, the speakers will therefore create a 60° angle relative to the listener; the ideal distance to the listener is set by the width between speakers.

Dolby Stereo

Dolby Stereo is an analog cinema format that was introduced by the Dolby firm toward the end of the 1970s. *Dolby Stereo A* is comprised of four coordinated channels. This is referred to as *four-channel matrix encoded:* one front-right speaker, one front-left speaker, a center-middle speaker, and a surround speaker in the middle-rear.

The rear channel is generally used as an effects channel—a cinema "experience enhancer," for example. The front center channel is often employed to create better film dialogue localization. Through this encoding, those earlier cinema projectors that could handle only two audio tracks now can decode a total of four. Near the end of the 1980s technical improvements meant that such sound reproduction could also work with less distortion and dynamic range. This newer system was called *Dolby Stereo SR* (SR for *spectral recording*). The four encoded channels are front-left, front-right, center (i.e., middle-front), and subwoofer/surround (rear).

Dolby Surround

This Dolby stereo system was further developed through an added surround channel. The now doubled surround channels were encoded with their phases reversed, and still mainly used as effects channels. The phase reversal means that any Dolby Surround signal is also compatible with normal stereo playback systems.

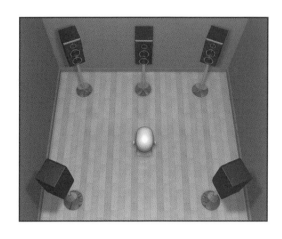

Dolby Pro Logic 2

This is another Dolby development that remains encoded for two tracks and is the direct predecessor of digital 5.1 systems. Though still without the 5.1 subwoofer, the first version nevertheless attempted to add true room ambiance via surround channels specifically set up for that purpose (left-surround and right-surround).

Dolby Digital/DTS (Digital Theatre System)

In contrast to analog systems that must be encoded in two channels, the *Dolby Digital* and *DTS* offer a cleaner digital separation of individual tracks. In a *5.1 system* (the ".1" stands for the subwoofer channel), each of the six channels feeds a single loudspeaker placement. The ".1" subwoofer channel plays a somewhat secondary, "non-spatial" role, as the human ear does not perceive much directionality with lower frequencies. The development of 5.1 has led to larger, more complex variations such as 6.1 and 7.1.

2+2+2

This system is something very new, and it provides a very different sound experience. Very simply, it allows for a convincing reproduction of an actual original acoustic environment, whether it is a jazz club, a cathedral, or an arena. Until now, the human capacity for three-dimensional aural perception has not been realized fully by any stereo system—until 2+2+2, which is the first to be able to provide convincing three-dimensional playback. This means that with this system, both the room and record-ed material are "transported" in their entirety through the studio and into one's living room.

Beginning Right at the Recording Scene

In recording in outstanding concert halls or churches, this system is based on six channels, which in conjunction with musical content, are set up specifically to capture the entire acoustic environment. Thus the 2+2+2 concept is bound up with the recording environment, with the end result that in a correct 2+2+2 playback, true three-dimensionality is reproduced.

Advantages

- Recordings can owe as much to their ambient sound as anything else, and are enhanced by a com-plete sonic canvas that includes the room.

- It captures a true acoustic (and emotional) representation of a recording location. Ambient length, breadth, and height remain part of the recorded ambient material.

- It offers playback that, in most locations in a room, provides the same quality without requiring a listener to be sitting in a sweet spot.

- The recording media are backwards compatible, and can also be played back with stereo surround (5.1) equipment.

Playback

The basic recording medium for 2+2+2 follows the DVD concept and multichannel capacity. To be able to listen 2+2+2 material you will need at least the following.

- A "universal" DVD player.

- A six-channel amplifier (i.e., six full-frequency spectrum ampli-fiers).

- Six properly placed speakers.

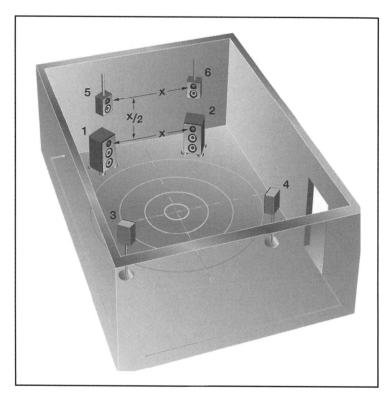

HARD-DISK RECORDING

This is the now well-known standard in recording, whereby tracks are saved directly to a hard drive or digital audiotape. There are, however, several different approaches.

Native Systems

Here, a computer employs sequencer software to control the recording process.

Stand-Alone Systems

In such cases, a recording takes place with equipment that provides a graphical display (i.e., a monitor) and controls independent of MIDI solutions.

Computer-Based Solutions

Here a computer is outfitted with one or more added cards (*digital signal processor* or *DSP* chips) that are in turn connected to external hardware. The computer functions in this case primarily as a graphical interface, and most of the processor intensive computations (such as mixing, plugins, etc.) are handled by DSPs.

Advantages

- Data is digitally saved and can be "resurrected" and further used or processed years later without quality degradation.

- The need for constant rewinding or forwarding of reels is obviated, which greatly decreases this aspect of working time.

- Individual recorded cuts may be copied loss-free and used elsewhere.

- Data security copies—without quality loss—may be made on various media types.

Disadvantages

- Audio material must be converted to digital format, which may lead to a loss of sonic quality.

- Recordings on analog tape are considered generally to be sonically "warmer."

Compressors and Related Effects

A *compressor* reduces the dynamic range of an audio signal, increasing the relative loudness of quiet moments while reducing that of louder passages. This can produce the effect of a signal with a louder overall level, which left in its original state, would have caused peak distortion or digital overs more easily. Compression may also give instruments more sustain, strength, and presence.

Applications

Some of the main situations in which a compressor may be useful are with voice or acoustic instruments during recording or in later mixing. In such cases, compression may reduce balance problems caused by differing microphone placements or when instrumentalists or vocalists produce different volume levels. Through compression, the overall sonic image may be brought into balance. Whether such compression should be used during a recording session remains the engineer's personal choice.

Advantages

- Compression can control signal peaks during a recording session. Nowadays, audio tracks are most often processed digitally, and initially compressing the recorded signal may greatly reduce the danger of unacceptable digital "overs." Many signal peaks are so fast and short that most metering, especially in computer software, cannot register them adequately. Thus, distortion may occur without being reported. Light compression reduces the need for peak signal reserves, and this in turn provides for a valuable increase in a track's average bit density. But in the application of compression, an engineer must be careful to know the machine's sonic quality.

- A further compressor application is in *summing work,* wherein a final stereo mix is processed by a compressor, in effect to increase the average signal level and create the impression of more loudness.

Parameters

Threshold

This determines the signal level at which the compressor should begin to work. Above this threshold point, the compressor begins to function by reducing signal level. The threshold is expressed in decibels.

Ratio

This parameter determines the amount of signal reduction over the defined threshold. For example, with a 2:1 ratio, any input above the set threshold would be reduced by a factor of two. In other words, an input signal 4 dB above the threshold would be reduced by 2 dB.

Attack

This determines the time in milliseconds before the compressor begins to function; this is also referred to as *response time*. Sudden peaks may be prevented with very short attack settings. The result is that a signal may sound broader and louder, but also "flatter," and audio material transients may be foreshortened. Usually improving dynamic control calls for attack time settings between 10 and 20 milliseconds.

Release

This is the opposite of attack. The time set determines how quickly the compressor returns a signal to its original unaltered state (i.e., after a peak has passed and the signal should be returned to its pre-compression loudness level). The shorter this setting, the greater the danger of the phenomenon called *pumping*—as well as the signal returning more quickly to its original level.

Soft-Knee

This is a pre-set switch offering typically two kinds of compression once the threshold setting is reached. A switch to a *soft-knee* setting applies a slower and much less obtrusive compression than a *hard-knee* setting.

Sidechain

In situations where an engineer wishes to single out particular frequency ranges in applying compression, he or she can employ this process. For example, to reduce the amount of compression in a range, one introduces an equalizer into the chain, and by EQing a certain frequency range, also reduces the resultant compression.

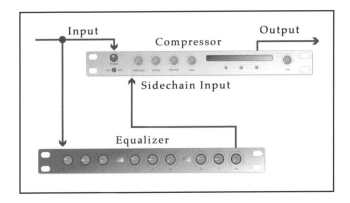

Output (Gain)

Because a compressor works by reducing a signal's overall level, this control provides the means to set the final output signal to a more desirable level—typically by increasing the signal to its earlier average loudness.

A Word to the Wise

Compressing a signal excessively creates a rather "rigid" or "narrow" effect. On the other hand, well-balanced compression increases the impression of loudness without damaging a signal's dynamic range.

Multiband Compressors

This dynamic processing is divided among several frequency bandwidths and is, in essence, variable compression applied to specific frequency ranges. Here, there are several additional parameters available to that of standard compression. With, say, a three-band compressor, there are three frequency ranges that can be compressed independent of one another. This kind of compression is often used in summing, where one does not wish to affect the entire signal, but only make needed improvements within limited frequency ranges.

5.1 Compressors

Theoretically, "surround" compression is comprised of six mono compressors, which are intelligently coordinated via a link function. This also works much like a stereo summing compressor just before the creation of a final production/media mix.

Peak Limiters

This is a special application of a compressor, where the ratio is maximized—essentially, it is infinity:1. A limiter is typically employed to stop signal peaks from creating distortion (such as AD converter "overs") or reduce feedback effects in a channel or in running a piece of hardware.

Expanders

The *expander* functions in the opposite way a compressor does—that is, it increases a signal's dynamic range, reducing lower levels further while raising the level of louder signals. This can be useful in lowering disturbing background noises. One sets the threshold just above the level of such noise but below the lowest level of quiet instrumental passages. The expander is often used in tandem with a noise gate.

Gates

A *gate* functions to turn off or dampen a signal when the threshold parameter setting is reached.

Noise Gates

A *noise gate* is an expander with a ratio of between 1:10 and 1:20; it is used to suppress unwanted low-level noises as completely as possible. In the modern age of digital hard-disk recording, however, the main use of this hardware—for example, the filtering out of problematic hiss from a guitar amp, especially at the beginning and conclusion of a track—is often supplanted through software processing.

Ducking

This is a special application of a gate. Using a sidechain input, the engineer creates a new signal path. It is usually a spoken track or one from a microphone, in the context of what is called a *voice-over* recording. In *ducking*, the gate works in reverse: A louder signal in the sidechain turns off the main signal, but when the sidechain speaker stops talking, then the main signal is returned to its normal level. Attack and release parameters determine the desired reaction time.

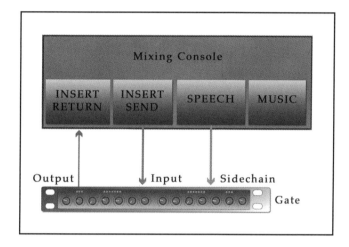

Frequency Selective Gating

In this case an engineer may introduce an equalizer to the sidechain/key input to further influence a gate's operation and/or response.

De-Essers

A *de-esser* is a specialized tool that removes undesirable sibilants and/or "S" sounds from voice tracks. In this modern age of digital processing, de-essing is very often employed immediately after the mic preamp stage, in particular to reduce strong sibilants (i.e., "s" sounds) that can lead to digital overs and inadequate headroom. These, in turn, negatively affect proper bit-sampling density and dynamic range.

This often consists of compression in the frequency range unique to such "s" sounds (8–10kHz), but is disadvantageous due to its effecting changes throughout the chosen frequency range, not just the "s" sibilants. This, in turn, may lead to undesirable lisping or nasality in the track.

Another very different process employs a selection of the sibilant frequency range in a signal, routing it through a phase inverter, and then mixing this signal with the original so that a cancellation of the unwanted sibilant sounds results. This has a great advantage over compression in its transparent, unobtrusive sound. The voice retains virtually all of its natural original qualities. In such cases, some de-essers have switch settings (typically, for male and female voices) that further define an operative frequency range for a particular voice type. Others offer an automatic threshold control that differs from the static controls typical of the more standard compressor. This provides for an automatic input level adjustment to account for differences in distance from the microphone, or whether a voice part is spoken or sung, while the chosen reduction amount remains constant.

Note that not only spoken and sung tracks can benefit from de-essing, but also those containing sharp sounds from cymbals or snare drums.

EXCITERS AND ENHANCERS

These processes add overtones to a signal through the introduction of controlled distortion. This can add additional high-frequency quality and presence.

Adding Sub-Bass Information

Through a phenomenon commonly known as *the missing fundamental effect* (also related to the phrase *residual hearing* in some psychoacoustic studies), this is a kind of subwoofer enhancement where it becomes possible to induce the mind to perceive beat frequencies made by differences in higher frequency signals as otherwise irreproducible low-frequency tones—that is, to create an artificially-enhanced bass response at, say, an octave below a given available signal. Such processing allows smaller speakers to provide the illusion of lower bass notes beyond their actual physical ability to produce these notes themselves.

Transient Processing

We refer to the first milliseconds (approximately 0–20 milliseconds) of a signal as *transients*. These are decisive in our distinguishing what the signal source really is (for example, whether from a piano hammer or a snare drum). If one were to foreshorten the transients, one could actually make it difficult to identify an originating instrument with certainty.

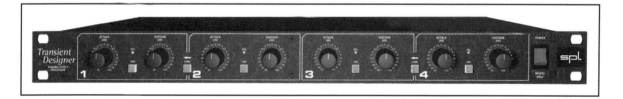

Parameters

Attack

Attack raises the transient amplitude and creates the aura of bringing a microphone closer to the signal source. The sound is more direct, has a stronger attack, and appears rhythmically more "forward." Reducing the transient level creates the impression of the instrument being farther away.

Sustain

This determines a signal's decay time in, for example, the foreshortening of the decay of a floor tom. Other past solutions used to achieve this end—such as noise gates—sound rather unnatural. When used to increase the sustain of a piano's signal, this provides for a more vibrant and/or expansive sonic impression.

Reverb and Related Effects

How Does Reverb Work?

A signal sends sound waves in all directions throughout a room. Reflections on walls, ceiling, floor, and various objects in a room immediately follow. The result is a myriad of reflections, which after a short time (50–100 milliseconds) mix with each other. The sum of these reflections creates the room's sonic impression; this is also perceived as a lengthening of the original signal, or a sustain effect.

With each reflection, a part of the signal is absorbed—its energy diminishes—and another part of it is further reflected in different directions. Naturally, the reflections themselves are again reflected and dispersed throughout the room until they disappear altogether; this process is called *signal decay*.

The accepted definition of this signal decay is measured in the time it takes for a signal to fall to 60 dB below its originating signal level; this is referred to as RT60. The first reflections that the ear can differentiate are the early reflections discussed much earlier, which determine in large part the perception of room size and relative signal loudness. In addition, these factors are particularly important in how the sonic quality of a room or hall is judged. In the open air, one perceives virtually no reverberation even though there may be *delays* (echoes) due to reflections from nearby surfaces—in a mountain valley, for example, or from house or building walls.

Reverb via Plugins or Hardware

Specifically constructed algorithms form one basis for adding the qualities of reflection and sustain to an extremely *dry* signal (i.e., one devoid of any room reflections).

Plugins

Plugins are dependent upon the processing power of a local system. Because of today's available computer power, there are excellent reverb plugins. The best algorithms, however, tend to be reserved by manufacturers for the most advanced hardware.

Hardware

Though separate cards have optimized routines and can usually outperform plugins, outboard reverbs have their own internal processors and can execute highly complex algorithms in real time. Price and quality differ greatly. For cutting-edge cards and machines, there are already a number of very good, "limited-editions" that perform well. Moreover, there are reverb machines that have their own very distinctive sounds, that today—years after their introduction—are still much sought after (for example, the EMT250, which is a classic for vocals). Alternatively, there are also those that emulate qualities of a characteristic recording epoch—for example, the AMS RX 16.

Natural Reverb

One can place a speaker in an actual room and record its signal with the added room acoustic. This may result in getting the best of both worlds through the added sound of a fine room—something that machines cannot duplicate. The process is, however, not flexible and most often done in mono.

Two Types of Artificial Reverb

"Naturally Copied" Reverberation

One can add to a dry signal through effects machines and/or presets a reverb that simulates rooms from small to very large.

Effects Reverb

There are two types of reverb that don't occur in nature, but are accessible via artificial means: *gated reverb*, whereby extended reflections are truncated through a noise gate, and *reverse reverb*, whereby the reverb is reversed.

Applications

Standard Reverb

This is suitable for vocals, melody, and solo instruments.

Plate Reverb

With this type of reverb, the sound is neutral, unobtrusive, and slightly metallic. It's suitable for brass fills and riffs, rhythm guitar, and percussion.

Gate Reverb

This is a "special effects" variety suited for snare and percussion.

The Three Most Important Parameters

Pre-Delay

This is the amount of time that transpires until the first reflections reach the ear—in other words, this is the time it takes for the initial reverb to be built up. The parameters are based on room size and on distances to the walls, which create the various wave reflections. The pre-delay parameter is principally responsible for creating the impression of room size.

Decay

Decay comprises the length of time a reverb sounds, or the time it takes for the reverb to die out. This is a decisive element in determining a room's sonic character. In essence, the larger the room, the longer the reverb time, although objects that might be in the room itself are also important factors.

Hi-Decay

This is the speed with which higher frequencies simply die out. Higher frequencies tend to dissipate more rapidly than lower frequencies.

Additional Important Parameters

Early Reflections

These are the first reflections that our ears are able to distinguish. When reflections reach a certain point of being mixed together, this is referred to as the *diffuse field*. Early reflections themselves determine the character of a room, including its size and even the elements of its material construction.

Reverb Time

This is the length of time of the reverb.

Wet/Dry

This refers to the proportion of the mixed original and reverbed signal.

Specific Rooms

Small Room

The reverb time is about 0.4 seconds; the pre-delay is about 20–40 milliseconds.

Church

The reverb time is about 4.5 seconds (large churches can be up to 12 seconds or more); the pre-delay is about 200 milliseconds.

Tips

- The more detached the musical style, the shorter the reverb tends to be.

- To position instruments deeper into a mix, one should record in smaller rooms and not use pre-delay.

- When one uses a larger pre-delay value, one may receive the impression of being nearer to a sound source. One example is a voice in the mix: In order to bring a singer forward, one should apply a longer predelay time.

- A song with a slower tempo may be more suited to a higher decay value (for example, 3 seconds).

- The shorter the reverb, the more "brilliant" it will sound. To create an unobtrusive reverb, one should typically choose a higher decay value.

"Convolution Reverb" (A.K.A. Sampling Reverb)

In this type of reverb, one may make a "fingerprint" of a room and apply it to a signal. The room is in essence "sampled." The signal should be recorded by the most neutrally sounding available microphone so that only a pure impulse return remains. Through this returned impulse, one may apply a process of convolution based on the mathematical principal of Fourier transformation, and thereby lend the original room reverb characteristics to the signal.

Advantages

- The reverb character of very expensive effects machines—indeed, of existing room types—may be simulated.

- Fewer CPU resources are required than by normal reverb plugins that function by creating reverb via specific algorithms.

Disadvantages

- In comparison to a calculated reverb, the convolution principal may be rather rigid and limited in its variability.

"Natural" Reverb

This approach uses large, very linear speakers placed in a room with good reverb (church, concert hall, bathroom, etc.) to play the dry signal, which is again recorded with the room reverb and mixed with the original. Electronic machines just cannot capture a comparable sound.

Chorus Effects

Chorus effects delay an incoming signal between 10 and 30 milliseconds and mix it with the original. In the process, certain frequency ranges are cancelled, while others are reinforced. The delay time is modulated by a sinus waveform in order to achieve non-static phase shifts. This results in a fuller, brighter sound.

Flangers

A *flanger* operates under the same principles as a chorus effect. A signal that is delayed under 10 milliseconds is routed back through the input feedback. Before the present-day availability of digital effects machines, engineers often achieved flanging effects through playback of the same signal with two synchronized tape machines. One machine was slowed down by simply braking it with slight finger pressure, and the speed difference created the desired effect.

Phasers

The term applies to an input signal that undergoes multiple delays of between 5 and 10 milliseconds, but is not—as with flanging—returned via feedback input. These delays result in continuous, frequency-dependent phase shifts that give the phaser its characteristic sound.

Pitch-Shifting and Time-Stretching

Pitch-shifting is the means whereby the pitch of an audio signal is changed either up or down (i.e., transposed) by a specific, selectable interval. In this case, the length of the material also changes proportionally to the pitch algorithm. In contrast, *time-stretching* changes the length of an audio selection and, in the process, alters the pitch. It is also possible to combine pitch-shifting and time-stretching so that, for example, one may alter the length of a selection but not the pitch.

The catch to all of this is that the larger the intervals or time shifts, the worse the sound quality becomes. However, most software is programmed with CPU-intensive algorithm functions that try to reconstruct the waveforms altered by "stretching" and "shifting"—with varying degrees of success.

Vocoders

For this effect, two input signals are required.

- A *modulation signal* (or *modulator*), which is usually speech.

- A *carrier signal*—for example, a synthesized sound.

The modulating signal is broken up and reassembled in certain frequency ranges. In the process, the carrier signal retains its pitch. The end result sounds like the well-known "robot voice." Musically, one can also use drum loops to modulate pad sounds in order to create special rhythm/chording sounds.

Increased speech clarity results from about ten bands, which are derived from and adjusted to those frequencies required for clear speech. There are also vocoders sporting up to 30 bands that offer much greater flexibility, although the higher the number of functional bands or ranges, the greater amount of noise there will be.

Distortion

As the name implies, *distortion* is the effect that simulates an overdriven amplifier. It is most often used in electric guitar tracks.

Leslie and Rotary Effects

The original "Leslie sound" consisted of a speaker cabinet that contained speaker(s) projecting into a rotating air canal or wave guide that directed mid-upper frequencies up through a rotating set of horns, which produced a vibrato. There are now multi-effect machines that simulate this sound and add adjustable parameters such as slow or fast speeds, motor stop or start, and bass and treble level adjustments. Their main use is with organ sounds, but modern studio and flexible electronics have expanded things to include the creation of interesting electric piano and guitar effects.

Delay (Echo)

Delays are used for doubling or rhythmically enhancing a signal. Doubling occurs at 20–100 milliseconds, and rhythm enhancement is at greater than 150 milliseconds. Delays under 30 milliseconds create sound alteration but no perceptible echo effect. The shorter the time, the closer one comes to a sound resembling that caused by flanging effects.

Tips

- If one wishes to double an electric guitar, one can lightly process both (stereo) tracks using a hard-disk recorder, and through this small delay time create the desired effect. Both tracks should be separated widely in the stereo panorama, thereby achieving—especially with rhythm guitar—an excellent, wide stereo image. This kind of doubling simulates a chorus-like sound that is perceived as rather mechanical and static, and should not be substituted for a second recorded voice or instrument track. The effect may be improved by using a modulated delay, which constantly changes the delay time through a *low-frequency oscillator (LFO)*.

- Those who have an effects machine that has no *beats per minute (BPM)* or tempo indicator (and no song tempo delay synchronization) can accomplish the same goal by making their own time calculations (in milliseconds). This formula is: 60000/BPM = delay time.

Wah-Wahs

The *wah-wah* effect is created by running a signal through a band-pass filter with variable cut-off frequency, thereby changing the overtones comprising the sound. Depending on the machine, louder signals may have more overtones than quieter ones, or vice versa.

Auto-Pan

Depending upon the mixing console or effects machine, a signal in stereo or surround panorama may be moved. The control of such signals is either hardware- or software-dependent. Simple movement from one place to another can be initiated through a sine curve that may extend to a very free movement in or around the available positions.

EQUALIZERS AND FILTERS

The idea of *equalization* (also referred to as *static filtering*) was developed to counter deficiencies in transmitted signals. For this reason the process is referred to as *equalization*, or *EQ* in shortened form. An equalizer functions by raising or lowering a certain frequency range. If more than one range can be processed at one time, this is called a *multi-band equalizer* and, depending on its design, may be designated as a two-band, three-band, seven-band, etc. device.

One possible disadvantage with EQ processing is phase shifting, which will alter a sound's character (though high quality EQ design may use exactly these phase shifts to enhance sonic quality). When problems arise, they usually take the form of a muddy or much less transparent sound when applying an extra measure of EQ. In both hardware and software realms, there are equalizers that are set up to provide a definite sonic quality.

The best results in EQ come through the use of high quality designs with, for example, linear phase or *finite impulse response (FIR)* filters.

Shelving Filters

Shelving filters are EQs that affect frequencies above or below a specific frequency rather than on both sides of a frequency.

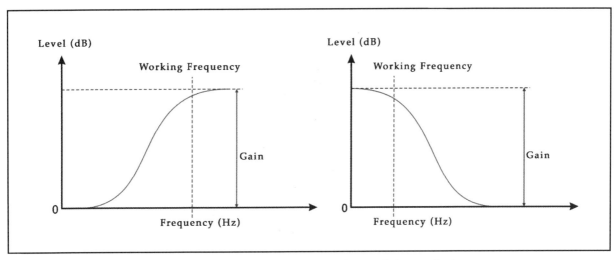

Shelving characteristics (increasing and decreasing)

This kind of EQ has two basic parameters.

- Frequency (expressed as Hz), which is the cutoff frequency, or the point at which the equalizer begins to function

- Gain (expressed as dB), which is the amount of increase or decrease being applied

Low-Pass and High-Pass Filters

These are "special case" filters that work to pass frequencies only above or below a chosen point. Here, the only parameter is the frequency at which the filter begins to work.

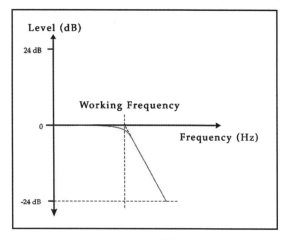

Low-pass filter

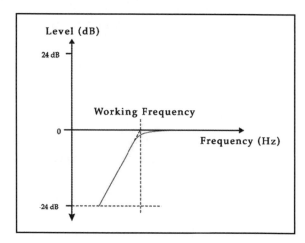

High-pass filter

Peak Filters

EQs with a bell-curve characteristic influence the frequencies both above and below the chosen central working frequency.

This type of EQ is adjustable through three parameters.

- Frequency (expressed as Hz), which is the central point at which the EQ is to function.

- Gain (expressed as dB), which is the amount of signal increase or decrease.

- *Q-factor* (or simply *Q*), which is the bandwidth or range on either side of a chosen frequency (i.e., its midpoint) affecting an increase or decrease in dB; a graphic depiction of such a working curve is called its *Q-value* or *slope*.

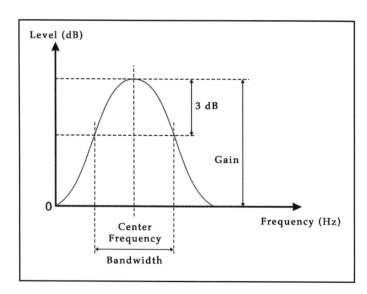

Peak filter

Constant or Proportional Q

These are two differing methods of invoking the way in which the Q factor is brought into play.

- *Constant Q* means that raising or lowering a signal at the chosen working frequency is not affected by the chosen bandwidth. This approach is ideally suited for adjustments requiring extreme precision, and is usually found in mixing consoles.

- If one wishes to use EQ in a creative, sound-manipulating way, *proportional Q* is usually the better choice. In this case, level increases or decreases are also contingent on the chosen bandwidth to be processed. The larger the bandwidth, the less the effect of the chosen, frequency-specific increase or decrease, and vice versa. A larger bandwidth will thereby automatically receive more moderate processing than a narrow one. This kind of processing is typically found in designs of past EQ generations. There are also EQ designs that allow switching between the two Q types.

Band-Pass Filters

This filter is, in effect, a combination of high and low pass filters. It allows those frequencies around a chosen central working frequency or frequency range to pass.

Notch Filters

This variant—the opposite "partner" of band-pass filtering—blocks signals above and below the cutoff points. This may also be achieved through simultaneous high- and low-pass filtering.

Filter Gradient

Equalization never completely eliminates a processed frequency, even within its main area of focus. In the case of band-pass filters, however, the frequencies that are increasingly farther from the cutoffs are progressively more suppressed. The amount of suppression or slope is measured in dB-per-octave, a value that is instrumental in determining a filter's sound character. Normally, this is around 6 dB/octave (also called *one-pole* or 6 dB). Cascading two such filters together yields a 12-dB (*two-pole*) filter, while one rated 24 dB would be a *four-pole* filter.

Filter Resonance

Filter resonance effects are achieved through special circuitry, which serves to increase the processing of those frequencies nearest the chosen working frequency and lessen processing for those away from it. If this resonance effect (also called *emphasis*) becomes strong enough, it can begin to oscillate at the chosen working frequency, a phenomenon called *self-oscillation*.

Passive Equalizers

This is an EQ type built from passive components such as *inductors* (coils) and high-grade capacitors. There are no op-amps needed in any of the EQ circuitry itself. Active electronics (transistors, integrated circuits [ICs], tubes) are only required in input or output (pre- or makeup-) gain amplifiers. Such equalizers depend upon extremely high-grade, close tolerance components, and thus tend to be very expensive.

Active Equalizers

Such EQ designs employ a separate amplifier at each available band that can increase a signal level, and each band's amplifier has its share of transistors, ICs, and/or tubes that work without influencing the others.

Graphic Equalizers

This term describes an EQ design that provides for multiple active band-pass filters that run simultaneously. These typically run in fixed intervals centered on octave or one-third octave points, usually on ISO standard frequencies. Some manufactures may add or subtract filter bands depending on the application of the graphic equalizer.

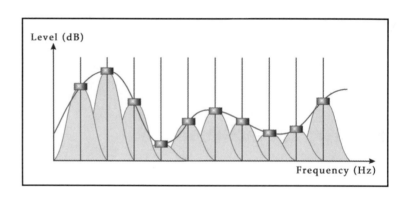

The different frequency bands are controlled by a series of sliders that can raise or lower a band's signal level. The visual arrangement of these sliders yields a graphic "image" of the chosen frequency adjustment(s). However, such graphic EQs employ bell curves in each band that can be increased or lowered and, if used incorrectly, neighboring bands can interfere with each other, causing comb distortion.

Half- and Fully-Parametric EQs

With *fully-parametric* EQs, all parameters (frequency, Q, gain) are independently adjustable. With the *half-parametric* EQs, there is no Q control.

Tube EQs

A *tube equalizer's* amplifiers may employ tube stages in lieu of ICs or discreet amplifiers. Here, the design is linear, the tube is always a part of the signal path, and because of the considerably more involved component prerequisites in tube circuitry, it is often more expensive.

A General Word of Advice Regarding Tubes

A common misconception about many equalizers containing added tube stages is to call them "tube EQs." Such designs are in reality best to be thought of as solidstate EQs with added tube enhancement. Nowadays, tubes are often considered important for their sound-coloring character, but this is only conditionally correct, as it is also dependent on what kind of signal is being processed. Basically, a tube sounds *linear*, meaning that it tends to emphasize even overtones, which to the ear create a pleasing "softer" or "warmer" effect in comparison with what is often perceived as a harsher or aggressive sound from solidstate amplification.

Mastering EQs

There is no such thing as a "typical" mastering equalizer, but if one wishes to define such a machine, it might distinguish itself from traditional EQ by the following features.

- There is a higher voltage power supply instead of the traditional +/- 15 V. The advantage is that a higher bus voltage can reduce the chance of clipping—there is an increased working dynamic range and headroom before clipping can set in.

- Class A design circuitry is present, which allows for reduced internal noise and distortion. Dual transistors are used in the power supply (one for positive and one for negative phase) instead of a single transformer. Even though there may be no signal present, there is a so-called idle current flowing in an electronic device. The design of Class A machines ensures that a full voltage potential is present in both transistors, whereas with the Class B design, the supply alternates between the two and leads to distortion at the crossover point. The disadvantage to the Class A circuitry, however, is that there is high heat dissipation, making the machine run hot.

- There are discreet components—high-grade, stable, components such as diodes, transistors, and resistors. There is no integrated circuitry.

- There are *detented potentiometers*, or controls that have fixed frequency settings (i.e., switches or notches) that provide for exact fine-tuning. This precise adjustment offers an exact return to previous settings

- There is complete recall function via such recorded presets whereby a session setup can be stored and again recalled when needed.

- Very large frequency ranges can be processed—depending upon the machine design, from 1Hz to 500 kHz.

- There are very low noise levels.

- Direct current coupling amplifiers are in use. Between the individual amplifier stages, there are no other components to influence the sound

- Very high-grade components and circuits are used.

METERS AND MEASUREMENTS

Peak Meters

With a *peak*—i.e., maximum signal level—*meter*, one can measure and view graphically a pitch signal's level. This is useful to guard against overs, which will cause distortion in the mix. A peak meter can trace and show the highest signal level at a given moment. In analog signals, this consists of what is called an *integration time*—which is about 10 milliseconds—to register a peak, whereas through exact samples in the digital realm this figure is less than 22 microseonds.

The above means that if one were to compare an analog and digital signal in such a setup, the level shown by a digital signal would be around 2 to 6 dB higher.

VU Meters

A *volume unit (VU) meter* logarithmically measures signal level. To function properly—so that the indicator doesn't constantly overreact—such meters are heavily damped, and therefore have a certain built-in imprecision. Very short peaks—typically 300 milliseconds—are easily missed.

Stereo Correlation Meters

Stereo playback consists of right- and left-channel information. This device measures and displays the phase relationship between two such stereo channels. Mono signals are displayed with a value of 1. Properly mixed stereophonic information normally displays a value varying between 0.2 and 0.7.

Single-channel information displays a value of 0. In cases where there is a phase error, the display will indicate steady negative values. Such a signal will not be mono-compatible, and playing such a signal as a mono mix will produce frequency-specific cancellations. In the case of analog tracks for vinyl record mastering tracks, not ensuring that the proper stereo correlation is present can cause serious problems in the final manufacturing production process, in particular for lower frequencies.

Goniometers

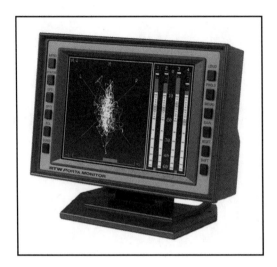

A *goniometer* displays the phase relationship of two stereo channels in an image reminiscent of a dynamically changing piece of steel wool. The ellipse-shaped display figure usually portrays mono signals as narrow, denser forms, while stereo information produces more rounded images.

Spectrum Analyzers

With spectrum analyzers, audio signals of about 20Hz–20kHz are divided into individual bands (typically, 31), analyzed, and shown via LED displays. This is mainly a support device, and it should not be thought of as a replacement for monitoring. The display reports information about frequency ranges in the signal, comparative proportions in sonic components of the entire sound image, and specific unwanted noises in given frequency ranges. With smaller near-field monitors that lack a full bass frequency response, this optical display may assist with control in areas such as EQ. The spectrum analyzer is also used in appraising various sonic aspects of studio speakers.

MIXING

Preparation for Mixing

- Label individual mixer channels to create a clear and accurate overview.

- Carefully organize your audio output tracks, and particularly the various busses. Typical busses might be set up for multiple vocal or guitar tracks, and always when multiple effects processors or EQ setups are to be employed.

- Thoroughly check to ensure that effects, plugins, and any other outboard equipment will be adequate for your mix.

- Ensure the proper methodology and preparation for summing compression. Do your first trials in bypass mode.

Procedures

Depending, of course, on the musical and stylistic audio content, the following mixdown sequence is highly recommended.

1. Drums (first the bass drum, and then the snare and the rest)

2. Bass (note that this is often mixed in conjunction with the bass drum)

3. Guitars

4. Vocals

5. All remaining instruments

For actual (i.e., not sampled or synthesized) instruments and voices, consider completing your *dynamics processing* (compression, gate, EQ, etc.) before bringing in other effects such as reverb.

After a mix is through with the above steps, one then employs automation, which puts the final touches on a mix.

A Few Mixing Tips

Mono Compatibility

Although it seems that there are fewer and fewer playback setups with mono switches or speakers, these are and will remain excellent means of checking and controlling the entire sound image during mixdown. Regardless of possible losses in audible higher frequency ranges, regularly switching to a mono mix and listening carefully to it can be of crucial help in giving an engineer a much clearer image of a properly compatible overall mix. A rule of thumb to follow is that a good mix—whether in stereo, surround, or 2+2+2—will also sound good in mono.

Moreover, from the standpoint of production, and especially for those who record for vinyl, it is a must to maintain mono compatibility.

Finding Resonance Middle Points with EQ

One can use EQ to look for and localize a resonance middle point that may be responsible for problem coloration. This functions best, however, with instruments that are largely non–pitch-specific, such as drums or general percussion.

Here's the process.

1. Listen to the solo channel.

2. Set a narrow EQ bandwidth (i.e., a high Q-factor) and a high gain increase.

3. Start at the low end of the available EQ frequency range and slowly move through to the higher frequencies. Be careful with your ears, as the amount of gain used can necessitate a very high and possibly dangerous playback level!

4. As you progress through the frequency range, you should be able to find the particularly emphasized overtones you wish to control.

An Application: Frequency "Overlap"

Should two instruments in the same frequency range overlap, so that the quality of each fails to be present, or it becomes difficult to discern one from the other, the process of finding the resonance points of one can mean the ability to bring it forward by further emphasizing it or reducing the overlapping frequencies of the other. Such a procedure can greatly enhance an overall sonic image.

The alternatives to the above are as follows.

*   Play other voicings or inversions of the chords.

*   Transpose a pitch up or down an octave.

*   Choose differing sounds.

*   Change or transpose the entire musical piece by, for example, a half tone.

Table of Frequencies

Characteristics	Frequency Range	Overemphasis
Sub-Bass	40–80 Hz	Boomy
Warmth	250–500 Hz	Muddy Sound
Presence	5–10 kHz	Coarse or Aggressive
Brilliance/Transparency	10–20 kHz	Clashing

Adjustment to Sound (Applying EQ)

It is always prudent to consider lowering those frequencies that are problematic rather than to attempt to increase those that seem lacking. In the latter case, the tendency is to create problems for the entire sound palette rather than to remove just those frequencies causing difficulties.

Different Reverbs

In a very complex mix, one should consider working with more than one kind of reverb setting so that the various instruments and voices may be invested with their own characters and optimal mix positions. Typically, there may be one type of reverb for drums, a more general one for instruments such as keyboards and guitars, and a special reverb or delay for the principle singer. With various kinds of special equipment there may also be the possibility—within a generated room type—to use reverb and early reflections to place various instruments in different mix positions. Today, it is common to hear a definite decrease in the amount of reverb used among recording releases, but there are also many recording rooms now that sound "dry" and more "precise" than in the past. Without reverb or room presence, instruments would sound much too "close together," and the mix would have a flat, narrow sound quality.

When possible, add less of the high frequency component in reverb, as this is much less obtrusive while still fitting the bill. Moreover, be especially careful to keep early reflection settings in mind, which alone are enough to give the impression of having added adequate room reverb.

Sound Distribution for Depth Perception

Through the use of console panning controls, an engineer can place a signal in a desired left-right stereo field location. With sound distribution for depth perception, one perceives the actual *depth* (nearness or distance) of various instruments based on the displacement and arrival time of room reflections. This is yet another method to maintain a mix's quality of "air" and transparency. More important signals that are positioned more closely are emphasized, while those less important may be moved into the background. The fundamental prerequisite for this is an optimally recorded instrument track that exhibits inherently good dynamic range.

Here are three ways in which this general concept can be applied.

Via Adjustments to Signal Level

We perceive near sounds as louder than those that arrive from a distance. With orchestra recordings, the engineer may move an instrument forward in a mix by employing a spot mic and increasing its signal level. Such mics pick up just a few room reflections simply because they are closer to the instrument. In such cases, it becomes important to monitor the track so that the instrument's sound remains natural. There is a trick to this: By using an effects machine, one can add a "touch of room" to the mic's otherwise too-present quality.

Via Differences in Reverb Quantity

The more reverb a sound has, the more its tendency is to sound distanced. If one switches an instrument channel to pre-fade and lowers its level while its added reverb component remains at the same level, the original instrument signal retains a lower level. Through this procedure, the impression of an instrument that is further back in the room or mix is created.

Via Equalization

Signals that originate at longer distances from the human ear are perceived as duller because they arrive with fewer high frequency components. Thus, the sound appears to be closer or farther away.

Via Microphone Positioning

Keep in mind that microphone placement can have an important influence on depth and spatial perception.

Separation and Width Through Panning

Separation

One can effectively EQ certain frequencies of overlapping instruments by moving them to different parts in the mix panorama, thus reducing the need for specific EQ processing.

Width

Typically, a stereo panorama has a width of about 80 degrees. Psychoacoustic effects, which employ phase shifts, can enhance this width considerably. However, the signal will no longer be mono-compatible.

Here's another tip: One may double a signal (through a duplicate guitar track that is moved to the left and right of a stereo mix, for example) and thereby enhance the overall stereo width.

Issues of Relative Loudness

If one wishes to check on the relative signal loudness, an effective method is to switch the mix to mono and listen to it at an extremely light level. If in this instance all levels appear to be in order, the entire mix should be so as well.

Monitoring Loudness Issues

Too Much Loudness

With some songs, one may get lost in the idea that more loudness provides more emotional impact. If one loses perspective this way, one will create a mix that contains many errors in EQ and proper dynamic range.

Too Little Loudness

It is sometimes tempting, depending on a mix, to allow for too few highs or bass components to be present.

Shortsightedness through monitoring a signal at levels that are too loud tends to damage one's ability to perceive proper timings in percussion tracks or to react correctly to added effects.

Monitoring

It is very advisable in any situation not only to mix with the best possible speakers, but to also use a small monophonic speaker or hi-fi setup to make quick comparisons. These are often called *bad references*. Through listening in these conditions, one can also gain an immediate idea of how a listener might hear the mix.

The Fletcher-Munson Effect

Different frequency ranges are perceived differently by the human ear. The ear is most sensitive in the range of roughly 3–4 kHz. Frequencies above and below this area must be louder in order to be perceived at the same level as those in the 3–4 dB range. Experiments have shown that the optimal loudness in mixing occurs at around 85 dB. This is loud enough to balance deficits in the hearing curve without encountering a substantial danger of ear damage. Continuously subjecting the ear to this volume level, however, will lead to considerable *ear fatigue*. It is crucial to keep in mind that in processing with an equalizer, one encounters the same loudness issues and problems that one does in working with adjustments to overall volume levels.

MASTERING

What Is Mastering?

Mastering is the final creative step in the recording and mixing process, during which the engineer puts the finishing touches on a stereo mixdown to arrive at the best possible overall sound for a public release. Elements such as fine frequency equalization, volume level, and overall loudness are under close scrutiny at this stage. Any sonic changes are going to show up in the final mix, and individual changes will affect the entire sound canvas. The art of mastering relies upon an engineer's ability to make the right compromises at the right times, while avoiding making things worse for the overall sound with the changes. A second aspect of mastering is the technical preparation for the final reproduction process in the appropriate medium—for example, a CD or DVD.

Professional Mastering

Less expensive productions may actually profit the most from the work of a professional mastering engineer. Part of this is because, typically, such productions initially lack first-class equipment—decent microphones, preamps, processors, etc. Just being able to send an end mix through very high-end analog equipment can greatly improve a digitally-produced recording through considerable added analog "warmth."

Loudness

Loudness is generally regarded as a psychoacoustic term describing the perceived signal level of a sound wave. A louder (i.e., a more loudly perceived) signal is, in general, interpreted to sound "better." Optimizing this quality tends to lend a signal more impact, particularly in its ability to be heard amidst everyday extraneous sounds—traffic, nature noises while walking in a park, etc.

Dynamics and the quality of openness or "air" are often lacking in highly compressed mastering copies. In the further processing of such elements, undesirable distortion may creep in. In this vein, the mastering engineer must try to find the ideal compromise between loudness and sound quality.

Requirements for the Mastering Studio

- The room simply *must* have a good sound.

- Use the highest possible quality cabling.

- Use monitors that can yield full-frequency playback.

- Use high quality monitors and power amps.

- Have at your disposal analog and/or digital equalizers, compressors, limiters, and loudness maximizers.

- Make sure that you have an amply-sized hard-disk recorder for those cases where the final mix is delivered in digital.

- Make use of a master clock for precise, coordinated synchronization of all digital devices.

- Use high-quality D/A and A/D converters for transfers among different formats and to drive external analog equipment.

Subcodes

In addition to the purely audio data, a CD also must have *subcode* information so that players or computer software may perform their playback functions properly. Depending upon the medium, the subcode can include track durations, title markings, ISRC codes, added graphics or short video clips, copyright protection, and so on.

ISRCs

The *International Standard Recording Code (ISRC)* consists of a 12-digit recognition number for a CD title. This is added to the subcode during audio CD pre-mastering and remains a silent part of the production. If a CD title is used in radio or TV broadcasts, this ISRC code can be read and a license agreement, for example, between the broadcaster and label could be initiated more easily than through following a label code. ISRC codes can be applied for through the International Federation of the Phonographic Industry (IFPI).

Here's the structure of the code using the example ISRC DE-A44-22-00212.

- Recognition: ISRC

- Two-digit land code: DE (which stands for Germany)

- Three-digit proprietary owner key: A44

- Two-digit year code: 22

- Five-digit recording code: 00212

Appendix A: A Short Glossary of Basics

Amplitude—The maximum peak wave energy—that is, as measured at its highest central point.

Frequency (in Hertz)—The number of cycles a waveform makes in one second. One hertz (Hz) is one cycle per second.

Fundamental—The lowest note of a single pitch that, with the exception of pure, electronically generated tones, is comprised of other mathematically determined higher notes—called *overtones, harmonics,* or *partials*—that sound with it. These play a pivotal role in the color or timbre of a pitch.

Octave—The pitch that occurs at the doubling or halving of a pitch or frequency.

Period T—The time taken for a wave to complete its cycle and return to its original point.

Phase—Describes the placement of a pitch cycle in a given time frame. A pitch is comprised of two "+" and "−" halves of a period, and these occur along a timeline. If two identical signals are mixed but are displaced exactly 180 degrees, the value of this time shift is out of phase and results in their canceling each other out.

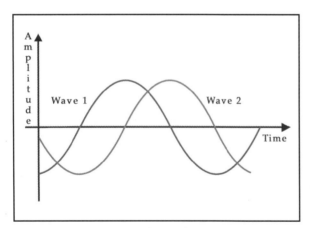

90° phase shift

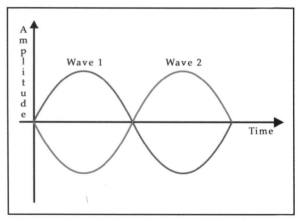

180° phase shift (canceling each other out)

With special filtering circuitry, one can create special time variations in a musical passage, which can be applied in various ways to alter tone color. For example, a snare drum may be recorded with two microphones that are combined in the desired proportions in the mix. If one, however, makes a slight delay in one or both of the signals, or shifts just a few milliseconds in time in relation to the other tracks, the result can have a completely different sonic quality and result from the original. Undesirable lower frequencies may also be subtly reduced. Through phase shifts, one may accent or cancel out entire areas of a mix's frequency spectrum.

Wave—Propagating air vibrations.

Wavelength—The actual size of a wave measured in the air.

APPENDIX B: CURING HUM

Direct-Injection Boxes

One always finds a DI box in action when noise disturbances in the signal path—especially hum—must be curbed. The longer the signal path is, the more the likelihood of such noises. With devices that have non-symmetrical/non-balanced connections (for example, synthesizer and guitar outputs), a DI box can completely eradicate problematic noises. The two types of these boxes are *passive*—the simpler variation that simply makes the signal path symmetrical—and *active*. The active type usually uses battery power and, depending upon design, can handle various types of inputs and outputs.

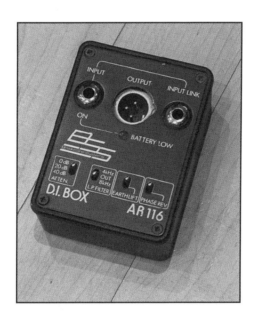

Ground Lift Switches

Hum can be a problem particularly where there may be irregularities or shortcomings in the power supply. A solution to this is by the use of a *ground lift*, where grounding may be separated from a common bus. One example of a situation that can cause a hum is a ground loop due to common connections between both a keyboard and guitar preamp. In cases where an instrument like a guitar does not have a power supply and might be connected directly to a mixing console, one should leave the ground lift inactive, as this can have the opposite effect, introducing noise which is at least as bad as, if not worse than, hum.

APPENDIX C: CABLES AND CONNECTORS

The basic prerequisite of a good cable is first and foremost the capacity to transmit a signal from input to output as accurately as possible. Depending upon manufacturer and pricing, one can find a lot of variation in cable quality. In a mastering studio, one should use only the best possible cable quality. Every connection from beginning to end represents a transmission point that can influence a signal, and often not for the better. Clearly, this can have an additive effect that should not be underestimated.

Cable Winding

Every cable possesses its own unique structural properties and twisting tendency that allows it—as long as this is not accomplished with force—to be wound gently. The often-seen winding about the arm and elbow often results in a damaged cable, and only proper winding guarantees a long life and dependable conducting properties.

Analog Cables

Electrons move easily in copper strands, transporting a signal from input to output. Every cable, however, has another property: resistance to electrical flow. This may be defined by the diameter and length of a cable. The longer a cable is, the more restricted its transmitting bandwidth becomes. Such restrictions first show up in higher frequencies. This problem may be ameliorated by cable with a greater diameter.

Damping

Signal intensity constantly dissipates during transmission through a cable. This is defined in a logarithmic relationship between signal outputs to signal inputs measured in decibels.

Insulation

Cable insulation consists of layers, including a mesh of copper and aluminum that functions on a principle derived from what is known as a *Faraday cage*, which provides shielding from electrical fields. Here, potential noise from such fields is routed to ground before it can affect audio content.

Symmetric or Balanced Cables

These cables consist of two wires that transmit the same signal, one of which is in reverse phase with respect to the other. They are termed *plus/tip (+)* and *minus/ring (–)*. A noise that gets into one line also gets into the other, and ultimately the two cancel each other out owing to the phase reversal.

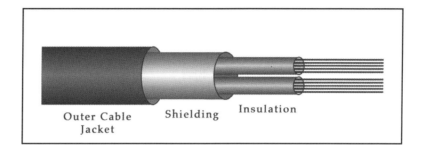

Non-Symmetric or Unbalanced Cables

These cables consist of a single wire for the signal. In cases where an unbalanced line uses a two-wire cable, both wires should be combined in one lead.

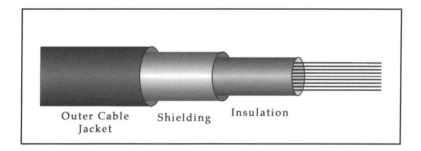

Digital Cables

Digital cables require an analog signal to be first converted into a digital stream. There are then two ways for transmitting this data.

Via Optical or Light Transmission

This cable type employs so-called *optical cables*, which internally reflect and retain a light impulse that it can conduct along its length to its endpoint, where a receiver converts the light impulses to electrical ones. This is the principle method for data transmission in an ADAT system.

Via Analog Cables

Transmitting digital data this way does not differ a great deal from moving analog signals along shielded metal wires, though similar considerations (resistance, insulation) also apply to a greater degree, making digital cables somewhat different. Professional users employ only balanced cables for digital transmission, where formats include AES/EBU, SPDIF, etc.

1/4-Inch Connectors

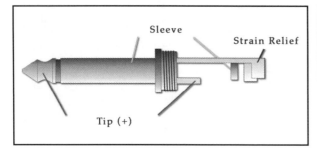

Non-balanced/mono

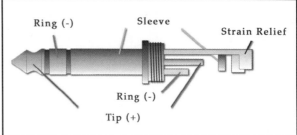

Balanced/stereo

When used with non-balanced leads, stereo 1/4-inch plugs should have the minus (ring) and ground (sleeve) soldered together at their wire connection points.

XLR Connectors

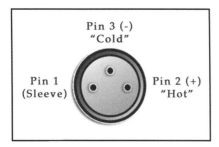

XLR connectors are always manufactured with balanced connections and, with few exceptions, should be used that way. Input jacks are female, and outputs are fitted with male plugs. This is the international standard, although it is possible to find equipment that does not conform to this norm.

XLR Cables

The insulating mesh should be soldered to one connector, but not to the other—this helps to reduce hum. This is a rule that generally holds true for all cable connections of this type, except those that are used with microphones.

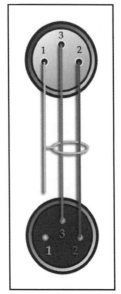

XLR plug (top) and jack (bottom)
XLR plug 1 (sleeve) not connected with XLR jack 1
XLR plug 2 (+/hot) connected with XLR jack 2
XLR plug 3 (minus/cold) connected with XLR jack 3

XLR-Phone Plug Microphone Cable Connections

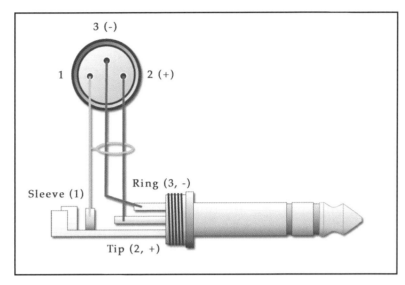

3 (-)

1   2 (+)

Ring (3, -)

Sleeve (1)

Tip (2, +)

XLR jack connected with balanced cable to balanced 1/4-inch plug

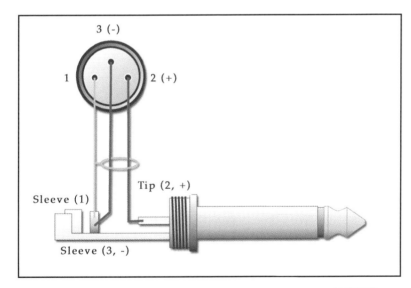

3 (-)

1   2 (+)

Tip (2, +)

Sleeve (1)

Sleeve (3, -)

XLR jack connected with balanced cable to unbalanced 1/4-inch plug

Multicore

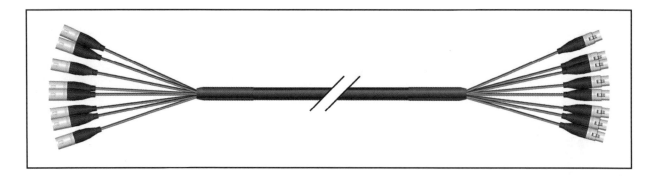

A *multicore* cable is one in which multiple individual cables are bound together. In order to minimize cross-talk effects, it is wise not to transmit both line-source and microphone signals together, as in such cases there will be signals with huge −50 dB and +6 dB level differences in much too close proximity to one another.

MIDI Plugs and Cables

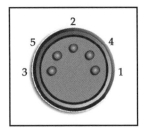

1. No function
2. Sleeve
3. No function
4. Data (+)
5. Data (−)

With MIDI connections, the only critical pins are 3 and 5; they must be connected one-to-one via their cables.

MIDI signal flow involves serial transmission, and therefore should be limited to cable lengths of 10 meters or less to avoid data loss, which is often recognizable by timing variations in individual pitches.

Optical or Fiber Optic Cables

In recording studios, this cable type, which is made out of glass fiber, is often referred to as *ADAT cable*. Typically, its connectors are known as *TOSLINK*.

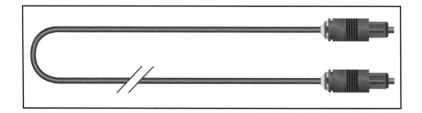

Tiny Telephone Plugs

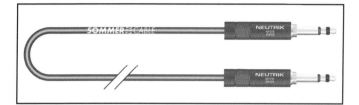

Originally these plugs—which are also called *TT plugs*—were designed and implemented for telecommunications applications for when an operator or technician made individual connections by hand.

Today such TT plugs function primarily with patchbays, as they are very durable and not susceptible to noise or other interference. Their appearance is much like a balanced 1/4-inch plug though much smaller, thinner, and with a more rounded tip. The smaller diameter of these plugs allows for a considerably greater number of connections when space is at a premium.

A Sample Soldering Project—Creating an XLR Cable

Tools and Supplies

- Soldering iron
- Lead- and halogen-free solder
- Solder-forming flux
- Cable knife, to remove the outer insulation layer
- Cable insulation stripper, to remove individual wire insulation
- Edge cutter (small and sharp)
- Cable tester, to check the functionality of soldered cable and plug joints

Procedure

1. Disassemble the XLR connector. This includes removing the cable shielding and all individual plug parts.

2. Remove the cable shielding portion that will no longer be needed.

3. Clamp down the XLR insert so that it does not shift while the soldering process is underway.

4. Remove the outer and inner cable insulation, taking precautions not to damage the inner wires, which can cause short circuits or unexpected transmission errors.

5. Remove the filler material; this is often a fabric or plastic lining.

6. Separate the shielding from the inner wires. Give them a slight twist, which opens the larger tubing.

7. Twist a portion of the shielding end to create a small, single-wire strand.

8. Remove the insulated ends of the two inner wires with the cable stripper.

9. Prime or tin the plug insert pins with solder, as this will ensure a better solder joint. An optimal soldering temperature with 4% silver solder occurs at approximately 320–340° Celsius.

10. Prepare the wires with solder-forming flux so as to establish better solder joints, and then prime or tin the individual wires.

11. Solder the wires to the appropriate pins. For an XLR, that means ground to pin 1, red/hot to pin 2, and blue/cold to pin 3.

12. Reassemble the individual parts and tighten the connector housing.

13. Test the cables with a cable tester or voltmeter.

APPENDIX D: PATCHBAYS

Patchbays function a bit like "traffic cops," enabling signals to be transferred flexibly among various machines. Generally, device connections are permanently wired at the rear of the unit, while on the front one has the ability with patch cables or switches to change signal routing.

Analog Patchbays

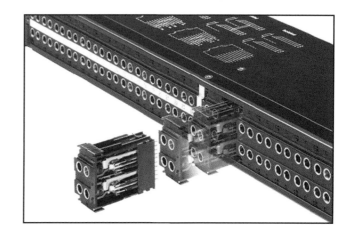

The front of the patchbay consists of two rows of individual jacks. The upper row is called the *source* and the lower is the *destination*.

On the reverse side, connecting cables from various machines are fixed either mechanically or by soldering. The margin for error with soldered connections is greater than for mechanical binders. Most audio patchbays have frontal connections that are either of the 1/4-inch or tiny telephone variety. Due to their small size, TT plugs provide for compact format, while 1/4-inch plugs are considered by some to be easier to handle and more robust.

Connecting Jacks

There are two types of connecting jacks.

Normalized Jacks

In these jacks, the shield, positive/tip, negative/ring are soldered to the connecting cable, while the two other available contacts serve as a bridge from source to destination.

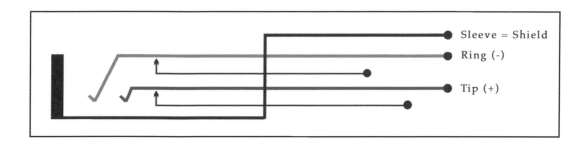

Sleeve = Shield

Ring (-)

Tip (+)

Non-Normalized Jacks

The shield, positive/tip, negative/ring are soldered to the connecting cable.

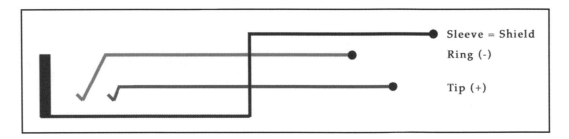

Configurations

There are four possibilities in which a patchbay can be configured.

Non-Normalized

The upper and lower rows are non-normalized. There is no connection between source and destination. In this way, a signal may be moved freely among various channels via a patch cable.

Fully-Normalized

The upper and lower rows have normalized jacks with source and destination bridged as shown in the illustration. Through the internal bridging of source and destination, there is a direct connection (obviating the use of a front-side patch cable). The signal is interrupted as soon as a patch cable is inserted into either the source or destination jack.

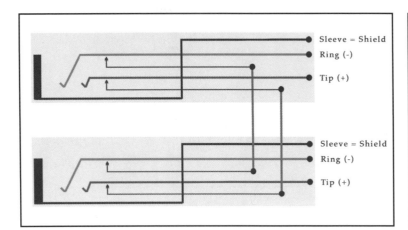

Half-Normalized

Here, the upper row consists of non-normalized jacks and the lower of normalized jacks, with source and destination bridged as shown in the illustration. Through the internal bridging of source and destination, there is a direct connection—a front-side patch cable is not necessary. The signal is interrupted only when a patch cable is inserted into the destination jack.

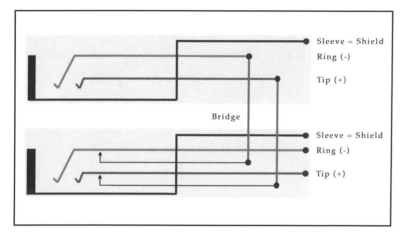 

Normalized—Special Configuration

The upper and lower rows consist of normalized jacks. There is no direct connection between upper and lower rows, but rather the normalizing bridge is realized via a *dual in-line package (DIP)* switch. One can employ a DIP switch for each channel regardless of its being half- or fully-normalized.

Digital Audio Patchbays

A digital audio patchbay is designed to route digital signals (such as SPDIF, AES/EBU, or ADAT optical). Here, frontal links are controlled by *potentiometers* (also called *pots*—basically, knobs) or button switches. Depending on the design, the rear-side consists of one or more of the specified digital connection options.

Manual MIDI Patchbays

The reverse sides of such boxes have MIDI-IN and MIDI-OUT jacks. Front-side faders provide various routings—i.e., which input is to be paired with which output.

APPENDIX E: MIDI

The Basics

By the means of MIDI cable connections, it is possible for two machines to exchange digital information. In principle, this information exchange deals with musical pitches (i.e., Note On and Note Off commands). Additional machine-specific parameters—for example, a type of effect for an automatic selection of specific sounds—may also be sent with the transferred pitch information.

In MIDI data transfers, actual audio waves are not transmitted, but rather only the control signals for pitches or for altering sound parameters. Every MIDI connection offers the possibility for up to 16 different, simultaneous pitches on each channel.

MIDI Transmission Protocol and Connections

Sending a MIDI command actually requires only one cable, but having two cables is advisable because one often needs a way to receive returning data. One connects the MIDI-OUT of one machine to the MIDI-IN of another, and vice versa.

The MIDI-THRU connector also offers the possibility of transferring data intended for one machine through another without the original data sent to the first machine affecting the message received by the second. This procedure can work for multiple, "daisy-chained" machines. This is less advisable because it can lead to signal delays. In this, help may be obtained from the so-called MIDI-THRU.

Modules

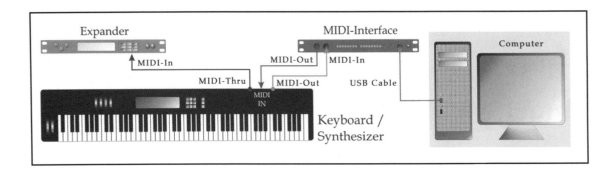

MIDI-THRU Modules

These devices route multiple outputs from a single MIDI input, each of which can send MIDI commands to separate machines.

MIDI-Merge Boxes

An opposite partner to the MIDI-THRU module is a MIDI-merger module. Two or more MIDI inputs are combined and routed to a single MIDI output.

MIDI Interfaces

Sequencers generate musical MIDI samples—for example, via a keyboard that can save such samples and later play them back—and, while most are software driven, one occasionally encounters hardware types. For this, one needs a MIDI interface along with a sequencer, the former being responsible for converting the samples for use in the computer. Some MIDI interfaces have only one input and one output, while others offer numerous connections. When installing MIDI drivers, so-called ports will be set up for every MIDI-IN and MIDI-OUT. An interface with eight MIDI-INs and eight MIDI-OUTs allows one to connect up to eight different machines. Each port has 16 channels available, therefore providing a total of 128 channels.

Mono synthesizers can play back only one assigned MIDI command at a time; this requires only one channel. *Polyphonic* machines, on the other hand, can receive multi-channel data. Each sound is assigned to a channel and can be played back simultaneously with the others. A machine that operates in this way is described as being *multi-timbral*.

MIDI over LAN

This technology is used so that computers that do not have standard built-in MIDI connections, but are needed for MIDI applications, may transfer MIDI commands. Special software is used to set up virtual MIDI ports on the network of those computers needed for the work. This available network serves as a conduit for MIDI data to be transferred back and forth.

Advantages

- One needs neither MIDI cables nor interfaces. In larger studios with multiple computers, this results in considerable cost savings.

- Pre-existing network connections may be used.

- This setup offers higher transfer rates.